Capturing Change

Creating Systems of Transformation through Continuous Improvement

Alex Johnson, PhD

Capturing Change
COPYRIGHT © 2021 Alex Johnson

All rights are reserved. No part of this publication may be reproduced, distributed or transmitted in any form or by any means, including photocopying, recording or other digital or mechanical methods, without the prior written permission of the author, except in cases of fair use as permitted by U.S. and international copyright laws. For permission requests, please submit in writing to the publisher at the address below:

Jennasis & Associates
441 W. Bagley Rd. #334
Berea, Ohio 44017

Printed in the United States of America
ISBN 978-1-7329322-2-7

Table of Contents

Introduction ....*page 3*

I. Change Management versus Continuous Improvement ....*page 9*
   The Origins and Benefits of Change Management
   Challenges with Change Management
   A More Comprehensive Approach: Continuous Improvement

II. Types of Change ....*page 21*
   Developmental
   Transitional
   Transformational
   Operations Interrelated with Change—Nokia

III. Foundations for Ongoing Change ....*page 33*
   The Plan-Do-Check-Act (PDCA) Cycle
   Concomitant Interfacing

IV. The Uninterrupted Cycle of Leadership Effectiveness (UnCLE) ....*page 43*
   Identify a Cause for Action
   Identify the Strategies and Tactics that Address the Cause for Action
   Measure Success against Internal Expectations and External Norms and
       Standards
   Introduce the Next Wave of Organizational Refinements and Innovations
   Potential Pitfalls

V. Becoming a Leader of Transformation ....*page 69*
   Leading a System of Transformation
   Personalizing Leadership
   Establishing Direction through Vision, Strategy, and Outcomes
   Building and Sustaining Your Foundation
   Authenticity in a Leader of Transformation—Howard Schultz

VI. Requirements for and Drivers of Change ....*page 87*
   Requirements for Change
   Drivers of Change

VII. Models of Change: Case Studies of Transformational Systems ....*page 103*
   Netflix (Digital Transformation)
   Ørsted (Climate Change)
   DBS Bank (Financial Technology)
   Philips (Health Care)

Lagniappe ....*page 121*
References ....*page 125*
Acknowledgement ....*page 137*

Foreword

In *Capturing Change*, Dr. Alex Johnson reminds us that change, no matter the instigator, is a constant. As I write this, leaders around the world are focused on navigating the vast disruption created by the COVID-19 pandemic. This book lays the foundation for embracing ongoing change and illustrates continuous improvement versus change management—a powerful concept that is relevant now more than ever.

The methods described by Dr. Johnson ensure long-term success by incorporating change into ongoing operations. He outlines a system of continuous improvement in which change is planned, deliberate, and gradual. Unlike common change-management models, his process is cyclical rather than linear. There is no starting or ending point, but there are intersections where an organization gains clarity about where it is and where it needs to be. Even urgent change, such as a response to a global pandemic, can be addressed within this framework.

Yet the process does not stand alone in Dr. Johnson's model. *Capturing Change* also emphasizes the need to develop "leaders of transformation." These leaders focus entirely on change for the advancement of the organization. They stay ahead of trends and push boundaries. They inspire and mobilize others to continuously create, implement, evaluate, and enhance. And as they confront obstacles, they go back to vision, strategy, and outcomes to rechart a course to transformation.

I have experienced the impact of this type of continuous improvement in my role leading Medical Mutual of Ohio, one of the nation's oldest health insurance providers. The company's longevity and history of success are the result of a longstanding culture of innovation and adaptability. Leading it through the many upending changes in health care requires flexibility, nimbleness, and a lot of creativity.

As a regional player in a very competitive industry, the company has worked to differentiate itself from its competitors, most of which are much bigger national players. At Medical Mutual, we had always treated our customers as partners—establishing unique collaborations, supporting community initiatives, and integrating them into our supply chain wherever possible. But a decade ago, I found myself thinking about how to push this further. How could we harness the power of our 3,000 employees, all of whom live and work in the communities we serve, to help our company and our customers win on a playing field of giants? That's when the program Mutual Appreciation was born—which effectively transformed individual spending into massive buying power intended to support member companies of all sizes.

The program has evolved and improved—a continuous process—and to date, our employees have spent more than $200 million with member businesses and nonprofits, all while steadily growing our customer base. And while I always knew supporting businesses that support us just made good sense, the impact has far exceeded my expectations. It has taken root in our company's culture, fostering a sense of pride and shared purpose. And most importantly, it's made a real difference for thousands of local businesses. I'd call that transformative change.

This book presents examples of other organizations—including Starbucks, Netflix, and Philips Healthcare—whose forward-thinking leaders have repositioned them to become "systems of transformation." In those organizations, like ours, change is natural, healthy, and welcomed. It leads to increased consumer loyalty and satisfaction, improved products and profits, and strong brand recognition.

I'm grateful for Dr. Johnson's leadership and friendship over the years. He has been a tremendous resource as we work together to continuously improve our organizations and our community. Using change as a tool for transformation is very powerful. *Capturing Change* demonstrates how it can be achieved.

Rick Chiricosta
Chairman, President, and CEO
Medical Mutual of Ohio

Introduction

"Without continual growth and progress, such words as improvement, achievement, and success have no meaning."

– Benjamin Franklin

In June 1752, statesman and inventor Benjamin Franklin ventured into a summer thunderstorm to conduct a scientific experiment exploring the link between lightning and electricity. As the familiar illustrations and stories portray, he flew a kite into the storm clouds to collect a static charge. This was dangerous work; at least one Russian scientist was killed a year later trying to replicate the experiment.

Franklin's innovation was to provide insulation by use of a silk kite string. A second thread of wet hemp conducted the charge from the kite to a house key connected to a Leyden jar, an early capacitor. He lifted his kite into the air and soon noticed the loose threads of the string standing on end and repelling one another in the rain. Reaching his hand toward the key, Franklin observed an electric spark. The Leyden jar was charged, and Franklin used the device to replicate electrical experiments such as igniting flammable vapors.

Franklin had proven that the powerful and destructive discharge of lightning was in fact static electricity. By successfully capturing that energy in his Leyden jar, he opened the door to the innumerable advancements that electricity has brought to our lives. His experiment led to the popular phrase "catching lightning in a bottle."

Nearly 270 years later, our nation is traversing a wide-reaching storm on many fronts. As this book goes to press, the COVID-19 pandemic continues to exact a devastating toll on people across the world. The capacity of health care organizations has been strained, the impact on economic systems has resulted in historically high unemployment rates, and governments have been tested as they attempt to respond to the immense challenges caused by the virus.

In the *Forbes* article "How the Coronavirus Pandemic is Accelerating the Future of Work," Heather McGowan reports that businesses had to change almost overnight, scrambling to secure technology to enable remote work and changing processes and methods at warp speed to prioritize the health and safety of employees and customers. McGowan suggests that these actions affecting work, learning, and daily life will become a new normal—that the pandemic could actually be a catalyst for transformation, an accelerant for existing and new ideas.

Possibly. But in the meantime, anxiety and uncertainty about the future cloud this forecast. What will be the ultimate impact of COVID-19 on our way of life? And can leaders at all levels respond to it? These questions are certainly hard to answer—but we do have a sense of the lasting effect of other worldwide challenges.

The Great Recession that took place more than a decade before COVID-19 had a consequential impact in many ways. For one, it caused Americans to change their spending habits: Many consumers turned to e-commerce, discount superstores, off-price department stores, and even dollar stores to secure merchandise at competitive prices. This shift in buying habits was catastrophic for some businesses, as more than 22,500 physical stores closed—with some, like Payless Shoes and Dress Barn, shutting down completely. Store closings have only continued as more consumers explore online retail and other purchasing options. In 2019, 9,300 stores closed, compared to 6,200 at the height of the financial crisis in 2008.

These significant store closings, according to Donald Sull in the *Harvard Business Review*, are perhaps a manifestation of a deeply seated problem: the inability to implement change appropriately. Sull concludes that leaders of besieged companies usually recognize a threat early, carefully analyze its implications for their businesses, and unleash a flurry of initiatives in response. For all the activity, though, some companies still falter. As Richard Kastenbaum notes in *Forbes*, they are unable to defend themselves against competitors armed with new products, technologies, or strategies; they watch their sales and profits erode, their best people leave, and their stock valuations tumble.

These failures occur, in part, because leaders often attempt to drive organization-wide change far removed from where it happens: on the ground. Kendall Lyman and Tony Daloisio, the authors of *Change the Way You Change*, believe this approach is counterproductive. They assert that change requires plenty of time and effort—and opens the organization to internal pushback and stifles growth if not done collaboratively.

The Value of Continuous Improvement

Some leaders are resistant to change because they have discovered that anticipating, planning, and implementing change is difficult—like determining where lightning will strike. There are numerous internal and external factors that must be considered to determine what needs to be changed and to ensure that the change is not only established but also sustained and built upon. So all change—whether sparked by the internal need for organizational improvement or an outcome of unavoidable external factors (like a financial crisis or pandemic)—is best implemented when the direction of the organization is clear, when it is in concert with the needs of key stakeholders, including employees and customers, and when risks are anticipated and prepared for.

The skilled leader of such transformation, therefore, must capture change, making it integral to the strategic and operational systems of an organization that treats it as natural, healthy, and welcomed. Because of this notion, I am reluctant to use the term "change management," which implies that change is only episodic and peripheral and requires separate strategies. Instead, I prefer "continuous quality improvement," often condensed to continuous improvement. This is the process of ongoing development at an organization in which change is contemplated, introduced, established, assessed, and built upon to improve products, services, and processes. I believe that continuous improvement is a more optimal way to operate in an environment where change is both constant and pervasive.

But leaders still need an approach to handle change in this manner. Just as Franklin needed to devise a system to capture the storm's electric charge without receiving a fatal shock, an effective continuous improvement approach must introduce change, sustain it, and build upon it within the organizational milieu. This is exactly what *Capturing Change: Creating Systems of Transformation through Continuous Improvement* is designed to address. This book provides leaders at all levels with a straightforward and reliable approach for recognizing and implementing change proactively in a continuous manner, incorporating such change into the culture of the organization.

Leading Change within Organizational Development

The nexus of this process is the Uninterrupted Cycle of Leadership Effectiveness (UnCLE), a self-propagating system of organizational development that I introduced in my book *Change the Lapel Pin: Personalizing Leadership for Organizations and Communities* and that I expand in this writing. UnCLE helps leaders obtain continuously desired outcomes. When built upon, these outcomes generate repeated success and organizational excellence. UnCLE incorporates change into the fabric of the organization as opposed to peripherally focusing on it.

The elements of UnCLE are cyclical rather than linear, interrelated as opposed to independent, recurring instead of isolated. Thus, the model is a fluid and interdependent approach to change that can be applied across an organization at all levels.

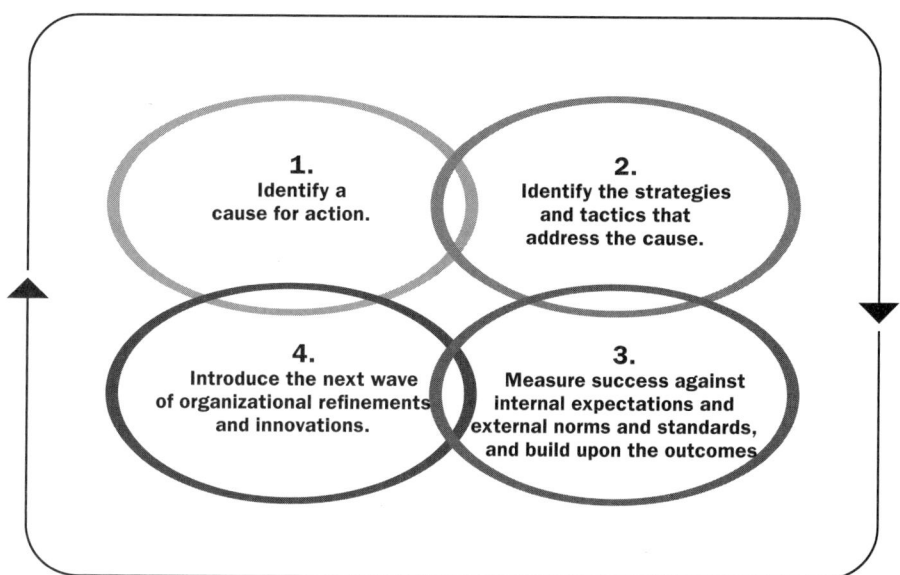

Overview of Capturing Change

Capturing Change provides leaders with the impetus to undertake change as an aspect of ongoing operations. First, it is necessary to develop an understanding of what change entails and why it is needed for continuous improvement. So beginning in **Chapter I**, I present the benefits of continuous improvement over change management. This is based on evidence that while change management systems have the potential to foster nuanced conversion, continuous improvement is a more natural approach to leading ongoing change.

In **Chapter II**, I offer greater understanding of change: how it is defined and categorized. I assert that the various types of change should be considered both individually and collectively to garner the best outcomes based on an organization's setting and need.

As **Chapter III** explains, this effort is most effective when an organization reaches consensus on what change is needed and integrates ongoing change at the level of business processes. W. Edwards Deming's plan-do-check-act (PDCA) cycle provides an example of this sort of ongoing change. In addition, I suggest that this change best takes place in the context of concomitant interfacing, which is the idea that all manner of change occurs simultaneously and that this confluence contributes to operational efficiency and transformation throughout the organization.

Chapter IV expands the UnCLE system. As disclosed previously, this is a unique approach to organizational development in which change is an important component. I explain each of the four elements of the model fully, offer directions on how to apply them, and suggest specific ways each element is pertinent to continuous improvement. Alongside this theory, I discuss examples of UnCLE in action through the development of the "One Door" model that has helped incorporate change into the culture of my current institution, Cuyahoga Community College (Tri-C).

This discussion is the backdrop for a more extensive treatment in **Chapter V** of the leadership skills needed to structure change within the context of everyday operations. This work is conducted by change agents who are familiar with continuous improvement principles and who possess leadership competencies built from the approach I introduced in *Change the Lapel Pin*.

In **Chapter VI**, I explore how change leading to organizational excellence is instigated by factors both inside and outside the organization that affect and catalyze change. Technology will continue to be a predominant factor, along with demographic and socioeconomic trends, government regulations, competition, and diversity as a growing attribute of the workforce. It is important that leaders understand the probable impact of these forces of change and how to respond to them.

Chapter VII brings these concepts together through case studies presented in the framework of UnCLE. These businesses, recognized among the Innosight 20, responded successfully to disruption and emerged as transformational organizations. They provide examples of how to capture change effectively in varied contexts.

Finally, I provide a **Lagniappe**. This Creole term is defined as "a little something extra" provided by way of good measure. My lagniappe is a summary of why I believe continuous improvement, combined with UnCLE and specific knowledge and expertise, is an approach to leading change that existing systems do not offer.

I hope this book will permit leaders like you to become more adept at understanding the pervasive, ongoing nature of change and equip you to effectively capture that change while drawing from its energy to create a system of transformation that leads your organization into the future.

I. Change Management versus Continuous Improvement

"Practice the philosophy of continuous improvement— get a little bit better every day."

– Author unknown

In *Organizational Change and Development,* Jeaw-Mei Chen et. al define organizational change as a process in which leaders work to optimize performance in reaction to an ever-changing environment. There are two ways that leaders can address this responsibility: change management and continuous improvement. To appreciate and apply the benefits of continuous improvement, it is necessary to understand how it differs from change management. Leaders need to know these differences as a first step in effectively establishing a culture focused on making gradual improvement over time rather than addressing change sporadically.

The Origins and Benefits of Change Management

Change management has become a universally applied term in organizational development. According to the Association of Change Management Professionals, it is the practice of applying a structured approach to transitioning an organization from a current state to a future state to achieve expected benefits. Lisa Kudray and Brian Kleiner suggest, in their article "Global Trends in Managing Change," that it is a continuous process of aligning an organization with its marketplace—and doing so more responsively and effectively than competitors.

Dean Anderson and Linda Ackerman Anderson, organizational experts on "conscious change leadership" and authors of several books, note that before change management became fashionable, leaders determined what needed to be changed and then delegated the implementation to others. Eventually, when transformation failed or became more critical, leaders surmised that success required their direct attention and involvement. According to the Andersons, this new insight gave rise to the field of change management—tangible proof that executives had recognized the need for a new approach to introducing change. The use of a specific management system could instruct a leader on how to attend to change more thoughtfully and carefully.

Ben Mulholland conducted an extensive analysis of the eight most popular change management systems in his article "8 Critical Change Management Models to Evolve and Survive." His results are summarized in the following chart.

Change Management System	Analyses
Lewin's Change Management	If you know that your business requires in-depth analysis and improvements, Lewin's "freeze-unfreeze" model is a great way to start. By digging up the roots of your methods and completely revamping processes and practices where needed, you can pivot your company at a critical time in its lifespan. Just don't try to unfreeze and change for every minor problem you find—it takes a lot of time and effort.
McKinsey's 7S	The McKinsey 7S model is best suited if you want to change for the better. You can analyze your current situation and draft changes to tackle the problem. This model is great if you are unclear about where to start. But if you are just looking to assess the viability of a specific change, it may be best to use a model that has a smaller scope.
Kotter's Eight-Step Process	Kotter's theory is great as a checklist, but it lacks the necessary back-and-forth (and, to a degree, actionable instructions) of a step-by-step process. Kotter should be supplemented with other approaches to make up for this absence.
Nudge Theory	Nudge theory is a concept that involves turning the people on whom your change most depends into the biggest champions of that change. However, due to this model's lack of specific, actionable instructions, combined with the required time and resources, it is best to combine it with another model that follows a set structure.

Change Management System	Analyses
The ADKAR (Awareness, Desire, Knowledge, Ability, Reinforcement) Model	ADKAR is a great model for cutting through complicated setups and getting straight to the point of how to improve your employees' reaction to change—as long as you already know what you want to change and why it is important. However, keep in mind that this model is severely lacking as a high-level plan.
Bridges' Transition	As the name suggests, this model is fantastic for guiding your team through a period of slow improvement or transition. Unfortunately, it lacks the heavy management that a large-scale change requires. In other words, apply this model to your core employees to ensure your change's success with the key players promoting it.

Mulholland found that each model frames certain aspects of organizational change. A few focus on monumental change and require a leader to know precisely what is needed to obtain it. Others emphasize process improvements across the organization. Some offer a step-by-step process that is best supplemented by more flexible models to improve engagement of individuals.

Mulholland also points out each model's limitations. He concludes that all are time-consuming and require additional resources and expertise that are often not available internally. Some are top-down approaches that run the risk of alienating associates by appearing not to value their expertise. Conversely, others are bottom-up approaches, perhaps making it difficult to attain high-level change. Still others are checklists, lacking specificity or real actionable steps, timelines, or conditions for advancement.

Challenges with Change Management

Anna Mar, in "Change Management vs. Continuous Improvement," believes that bigger risk-taking ventures requiring change management tend to be based on uncertainty. Mar suggests that this is not necessarily a bad thing. But according to McKinsey & Company, with 70 percent of transformations failing and 45 percent of companies being inexperienced in change management, leaders cannot afford to waste time and effort learning and applying techniques that may have little value. Most organizational change efforts take longer and cost more than leaders anticipate. Therefore, a failure can be costly and emotionally draining.

The challenge of improperly led change is compounded by the perceived issues associated with change strategies, especially change management models. One concern is that they rarely take into account the intricacies that coincide with wholesale change across the organization. Making this point is *Managing Change* author Bernard Burnes, who concludes that these models often focus on momentous transformation initiatives introduced at the highest level of the organization. Therefore, they may be too simplistic to handle both the transformation at the top and the required attendant change in the units, divisions, or departments where business processes need to be re-engineered or behaviors modified to achieve wholesale change.

Dinesh Venkateswaran, in his blog's appraisal of the popular model introduced by *Leading Change* author John Kotter, identifies another complaint: The steps in most change management approaches are linear, rigid, and incompatible with elements of other approaches. Such models inaccurately imply that the change process unfolds in a logical, rational sequence. Instead, change often happens in complex yet iterative ways in which the stages often overlap, are not time-bound, and may repeat within a cycle of change.

Yet another concern with many change management approaches is the assumption that core elements of the organization, such as vision and strategy, are not directly connected to particular change situations. As a result, these approaches may view identifying such core elements initially as unnecessary and suggest introducing them after the purpose for change has been identified. But according to the popular Mind Tools website—in a critique of Lewin's change management model—these fundamentals of an organization need to be evident, examined, and transformed where necessary to accommodate and sustain both extraordinary and routine change. Without this foundation, decisions about change will be possibly misaligned with both internal aspirations and external realities.

Furthermore, the periodic nature of change management means that while such systems may respond effectively to certain drivers (but not to all), ultimately, they do not achieve the level of transformation characterized in continuous improvement. Change management works to a point, but because it is for a limited period of time, it fails to achieve higher levels of transformation.

A More Comprehensive Approach: Continuous Improvement

I believe that all the benefits of change management, especially when one is dealing with monumental change or urgency, can be accomplished through a process that also emphasizes change within the context of organizational needs and operations. In this process, transformation is gradual and focuses on improving existing strategy, practices, and products. It is well-measured, grounded, and precise. Because it is gradual and anticipated, resistance is often not an issue, even when substantial change is necessary. Yet this takes committed leaders who believe that change is everyone's responsibility.

Not only does continuous improvement handle processes for advancing an organization, it can also address urgent change. The following chart demonstrates this effect and the difference between change management and continuous improvement in responding to drivers of change and transforming an organization.

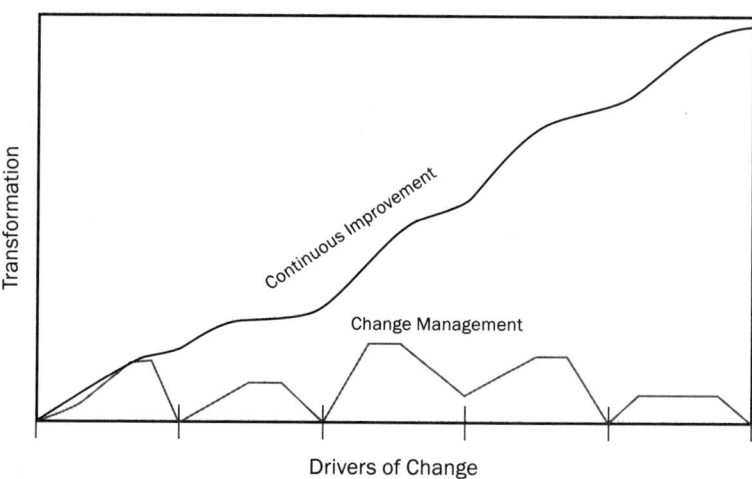

A brief example of this distinction is found at Toyota, as described by Lawrence Miller in his book *Getting to Lean—Transformational Change*. In the 1990s, the car company had an unacceptable rate of turnover among newly hired workers. It found that its technical systems, while based on continuous improvement, did not foster meaningful relationships between workers and supervisors. These systems needed to be redesigned quickly, but in doing so, Toyota did not abandon its reliance on continuous improvement. Instead, to improve employee satisfaction and retention, the company combined technical and human resource systems to create the Toyota Production System. According to Jimmy Smith, writing in *Peoria Magazine*, Toyota is now one of the most advanced companies with regard to continuous improvement. Its senior management is involved and supportive, but the company's efforts are driven from the bottom up, with work teams leading their own projects.

Toyota's use of continuous improvement is derived from the Japanese concept *kaizen*, introduced in 1986 by Masaaki Imai in his book *Kaizen: The Key to Japan's Competitive Success*. *Kaizen's* long-term focus has since been adopted by many organizations that believe any kind of change takes time, according to Elizabeth Douglas in "How to Develop a Culture of Continuous Improvement." And changing a culture, rather than implementing programs peripherally, can be a lengthy undertaking as well.

The practice of continuous improvement, however, has deeper roots in the work of W. Edwards Deming, who proposed a set of transformational theories and teachings that changed the way businesses think about quality, management, and leadership. Deming is best known for his pioneering work in Japan, beginning in the summer of 1950, where he taught top managers and engineers methods for improving how they worked and learned together. His focus was both internal, on relationships between departments, and external, on relationships with suppliers and customers.

As a trusted consultant, Deming significantly contributed to the dramatic turnaround of post-war Japanese industry and to business development in America. He applied his principles to the resurgence of the American automobile industry in the late 1980s, and he consulted with corporations such as Ford, Toyota, Xerox, Ricoh, Sony, and Procter & Gamble, whose businesses were revitalized after adopting his management methods. The Deming applications are numerous, but one that captures the essence of his method and serves as the foundation of his work is the 14 Points, as described in the following chart.

Create a constant purpose toward improvement. Plan for quality in the long term by predicting and preparing for future challenges, and always have the goal of getting better.
Adopt the new philosophy. Embrace quality throughout the organization by responding to internal and external customers' needs based on your quality vision.
Cease dependence on inspection to achieve quality. Eliminate the need for inspection on a mass basis by building quality into the product in the first place.
Move toward a single supplier for any one item. Quality relies on consistency—the less variation in the input, the less variation in the output. Rather than shifting production to the lowest bidder, develop trusted suppliers who meet your quality standards.
Improve constantly and forever. Continuously improve your systems and processes using the PDCA approach to process analysis and improvement. Emphasize training and education so everyone can do their jobs better.
Institute training on the job. To create a culture and environment for effective teamwork, build a foundation of common knowledge that allows workers to understand their roles in the big picture and to learn from one another.

Institute leadership. Expect supervisors and managers to understand their workers and the processes they use to help them reach their full potential.
Drive out fear. Allow people to perform at their best by ensuring that their ideas and concerns are heard. Use open and honest communication to remove fear from the organization by ensuring that supervisors are approachable.
Break down barriers between departments. Respond to the needs of internal customers; recognize that each department or function serves other similar areas of the organization.
Eliminate unclear slogans, exhortations, and targets. Let people know exactly what you want—don't make them guess.
Eliminate management by quotas and objectives. Look at how the process is carried out, not just numerical targets.
Remove barriers to pride of workmanship. Allow all workers to take pride in their work without being rated or compared.
Instigate a rigorous program of education and self-improvement. Encourage people to learn new skills to prepare for future changes and challenges. Build skills to make them more adaptable to change and better able to find and achieve improvements.
Make transformation everyone's job. Improve your overall organization by having each person take a step toward quality. Analyze each small step and understand how it fits into the larger picture.

Applying Deming's 14 Points has been shown to support transformation throughout organizations, large or small. Deming calls this process "profound knowledge" that a company uses to identify the external forces driving change and to lead efforts that result in transformation. The 14 Points, along with Deming's PDCA cycle (discussed extensively in the next chapter), are the mechanisms for carrying out this aim.

Despite their early popularity as management practices, the 14 Points were not validated as effective management theory until studied by John Anderson and his associates. These researchers synthesized Deming's writings, studied existing literature on the Deming management method, observed the method in practice at 41 manufacturing plants in the electronics, machinery, and transportation industries, and conducted investigations using path analysis to determine cause and effect patterns.

Their research confirmed that the principles were effective when isolating seven underlying determinants:

1. **Visionary leadership**—The ability of management to establish, practice, and lead a long-term vision for the organization by changing customer requirements as opposed to an internal management control role

2. **Internal and external cooperation**—The propensity of the organization to engage in non-competitive activities internally among employees and externally with suppliers

3. **Learning**—The organizational capability to recognize and nurture the development of its skills, abilities, and knowledge base

4. **Process management**—The set of methodological and behavioral practices emphasizing the management of processes or the means of actions rather than results

5. **Continuous improvement**—The propensity of the organization to pursue incremental and innovative improvements of its processes, products, and services

6. **Employee fulfillment**—The degree to which an organization's employees feel that the organization continually satisfies their needs

7. **Customer satisfaction**—The degree to which an organization's customers continually perceive that their needs are being met by the organization's products and services

Anderson's research has been replicated many times and has proven effective in several other industrial settings. A study published by Jack Marchewka in the *Journal of International Technology and Information Management* found the seven components beneficial when applied in information technology and health care. Marchewka recommended that greater insight into the application of the components may increase the likelihood of a project's success. This recommendation guided the research of Jesse Barfield and associates, as described in "Retesting a Model of the Deming Management Method." These researchers found that among the seven components, visionary leadership—when buttressed by internal and external cooperation, learning, and process management—has the greatest potential to advance both the benefit and effectiveness of continuous improvement.

Manus Rungtusanatham and his fellow researchers, following a study of Italian manufacturing companies, reached a conclusion similar to the Barfield team's: Visionary leadership is key to the success of continuous improvement. They found that leaders play a critical role in developing and communicating a vision that leads to a system of transformation. In this system, cooperation is an advantage. There is willingness to engage in learning, and it is easier to implement practices that focus on process improvement—and the processes ultimately support the continuous improvement of products and services. Understanding these factors is crucial to developing leaders who, as Dean Anderson and Linda Ackerman Anderson believe, move beyond the confines of change management to conscious change leadership.

II. Types of Change

*"Change your opinions, keep to your principles;
change your leaves, keep intact your roots."*

– Victor Hugo

For seven decades, Firestone Tire and Rubber Company's only challenge was keeping up with the steadily increasing demand for bias-ply tires as it sat atop the thriving U.S. tire industry. Then Michelin introduced to the U.S. market the radial tire, which was safer, longer lasting, and more economical than traditional bias-ply tires. The French manufacturer already dominated European markets, and it was clear to Firestone, based on its analysis, that Michelin could dominate the U.S. market unless Firestone responded effectively. The company invested heavily in radial production, building a new plant dedicated to radial tires and converting several existing factories. But although the manufacture of radial tires required a total commitment to much higher quality standards, the company adhered to its outdated design and production methods.

By 1979, Firestone was in considerable difficulty. The lack of commitment to new technology, dependence on dated manufacturing and production techniques, and headstrong leaders who refused to implement measures that were more aggressive essentially sealed the company's fate. This intransigence negated all of Firestone's intense analysis. Eventually, it surrendered much of its share of the U.S. market to foreign corporations and experienced two hostile takeover bids before being acquired by Japanese tire company Bridgestone in 1988.

As demonstrated in this case study provided by Donald Sull, simply understanding a challenge is not enough. Resisting needed changes or addressing change haphazardly can be calamitous to an organization and the individuals within it. To avoid this predicament and embrace change organically, consider Sinem Ikinci's article "Organizational Change: Importance of Leadership Style and Training." Ikinci points out that change requires not only recognition but also ongoing consideration in the context of regular operations to ensure that it is a natural, orderly part of an organization's growth and advancement.

Thus, change cannot be addressed only periodically during revolutions, like the introduction of radial tires in the Firestone example. Change must be a necessary and regular transaction, sparked by factors both inside and outside the organization that are acknowledged and welcomed. Change is a universal undertaking; it occurs across the organization and is introduced and enacted collectively at the strategy and unit levels.

When change is mandated, developments in technology will be influential in many instances. Also spurring transformation are certain social-demographic aspects of society, such as an increasingly diverse workforce and even political movements such as populism. These drivers and disruptors are discussed more fully in Chapter VI.

But according to John DiJulius, author of *The Customer Service Revolution*, the greatest inducement to change is improving organizational capacity to increase consumer satisfaction and numbers. Organizations can lose their competitive edge if they fail to consider new ways of looking at customer needs, delivering customer service, and strengthening customer interactions. Today, consumers have less patience and are more outspoken than ever before. They no longer tolerate subpar service, indifference, and unempathetic businesses. In summarizing this sentiment, DiJulius states the belief that only the businesses built on customer loyalty will thrive and emerge as market leaders for the long term.

Customers must be cultivated, especially among millennials, who are now the leading-edge generation of consumers and who present a unique set of characteristics and demands. For example, in the area of investing, this generation (when compared to other groups of investors) is more prone to change investment firms based on criteria such as overall satisfaction, economic outlook, and advisor productivity. They also have more options for investing, such as robo-advisors and self-directed platforms. This means that millennials—and other savvy investors—have more choices outside the traditional full-service channel.

Amazon is considered to be a model for customer service. Its passion for customer satisfaction has become legendary—and extremely profitable. In the article "Why It's Hard to Escape Amazon's Long Reach," Paris Martinez and Louise Matsakis refer to Amazon as the "everything store." In its dogged pursuit of growth, the company is dominating e-commerce and has extended its presence into diverse areas such as book publishing, media, retail, web services, energy, transportation, hardware, and health care. As a result, Amazon has become one of the richest companies in the world, and Jeff Bezos, its founder and CEO, one of the wealthiest men—all in the company's first 26 years.

The Amazon example illustrates just how beneficial it can be to understand opportunity and commit to a process for taking advantage of it. Within this context, knowledge of the nuances of change, such as types and systems, can lead to continuous improvement.

Change is not always epoch-making. It happens regularly, especially considering the many ways it is manifested. Understanding the various dimensions and types of change and their manifestations is important for several reasons. First, realizing that change is multifaceted acknowledges that everything in an organization is subject to transformation. Second, given that change is far-reaching, individuals are affected constantly whether they implement change or are subjected to it. Finally, although change can be typified, the various categories are interrelated and inextricable.

In summarizing these elements, two things are abundantly clear. Change is unavoidable; it will happen, whether desired or not. And consequently, a void created by unplanned change or unsubstantiated strategy can result in unfortunate outcomes—such as an environment that undermines morale, stifles productivity, or leads to the demise of an organization, as exemplified by the numerous store closings since the Great Recession.

This is why leaders must thoroughly understand how change can be effectively handled as an integral part of organizational development. This responsibility requires foundational principles, such as a vision for the future and the ongoing strategies and actions to effect it. Also necessary are leadership qualities that engage people, foster involvement and commitment, and lead to sustainability even through leadership transitions.

Dean Anderson and Linda Ackerman Anderson note that when leaders do not understand the type and scope of change that their business strategy requires, they cannot create an appropriate change strategy and consistently fail to get the desired results. Knowing which type of change is required is the first step in creating the right change strategy. In the ebook *Awake at the Wheel: Moving Beyond Change Management to Conscious Change Leadership*, the authors distinguish three types of change: developmental, transitional, and transformational.

Developmental Change

The Andersons call developmental change "improvement of what is." It is not only incremental but also planned. Unlike process improvement, which is ongoing, developmental change is occasional. It enhances or corrects existing aspects of an organization, often focusing on the improvement of a practice. Such transactions are regularly among the first steps toward instituting other more extensive forms of change. At the developmental level, the key is helping individuals understand why improvements are pertinent, providing the training needed to ensure that changes are understood, and seeking input from the individuals implementing the change on how it should be executed. Developmental change includes, for example, updating technology to support existing and prospective tasks, refocusing marketing strategies and advertising processes, and improving existing management processes and practices. The following examples highlight organizations that are represented in each of these categories.

Updating Technology to Support Existing and Prospective Tasks—Children's Hospital of Eastern Ontario (CHEO)

Dora Wang, writing in *Business Growth*, indicates that when the Canadian government made it a priority for patients to have access to integrated electronic medical records (EMRs), CHEO made the switch from paper to technology. A project team registered every patient, and health care practitioners at 75 percent of CHEO's outpatient clinics could order tests and document patient progress electronically. The process included the following elements:

- The primary team responsible for the changeover had a detailed, realistic plan.

- Another team's job was to educate and support health care professionals in their use of EMRs.

- Users of the system could attend practice sessions to learn how to use EMRs.

- The primary team continued to train health care practitioners after the EMRs went live, so users felt confident applying the new software.

Refocusing Marketing Strategies and Advertising Processes—Visa

Visa had to change its marketing strategy due to the weakened economy during the Great Recession, reports Joe Kelly in "Examples of Companies that Change Their Strategies." Previous advertisements focused on large, expensive purchases like cruises. However, during the recession, credit card customers increasingly used their cards for more common purchases, so Visa changed its commercials to depict people making everyday, less expensive purchases. Visa's strategy also included using social media applications like Twitter and creating the photo-sharing website Gosaic, where customers could submit photos of their credit card purchases.

Improving Existing Management Processes and Practices—Shell Oil

Given its size as a worldwide company employing more than 100,000 individuals, Shell needed more centralized operational management to ensure efficiency, interoperability, and agility in each of its businesses: oil exploration and production, gas and power, refining and marketing, chemicals, and trading and shipping. A post on UKessays.com reflects that the company was hampered by the following challenges:

- As a global enterprise, it had no standard controls.

- Decentralized project teams lacked shared methodology and experience.

- Processing voluminous information was cumbersome and complex.

- Mechanisms did not exist for sharing process-related knowledge across the company.

- Demand for support in this environment exceeded available resources.

Initial approaches to these challenges were inconsistent in terminology, approach, and structure. The company then enlisted the aid of consulting firm RevCom, which developed solutions consisting of a set of interlinked processes dependent on technology to integrate existing and new systems. Instrumental in this process was top-level support, with resources to integrate the system and provide guidance for users. Shell instituted the new management process in four stages:

- Empowered business teams to create useful process models

- Integrated resulting models with each other and with a core data model

- Communicated the new processes across the company

- Added knowledge through a process-oriented information management framework

Transitional Change

Remember, types of change are unique yet interrelated. Transitional change, according to the Andersons, "is the design and implementation of a desired new state that is different from the existing one." It requires management of the transition process to dismantle the old process or structure while putting in place the new. Transitional changes, the ones most people hear about, are those made to replace existing processes with new ones—such as corporate restructures, mergers, or acquisitions creating new products or services. Below are examples of organizations that underwent transitional change characterized by these categories.

Corporate Restructures—Microsoft

After the phenomenal and long-lived success of its Windows operating system and suite of Office products, Microsoft was struggling, writes Laura Troyani in *Business Insurance Magazine.* The gigantic company was stagnant and rife with turf wars between major business units that often viewed each other more as competitors than partners.

Innovation was being thwarted by a toxic environment that kept the company increasingly dependent on regular refresh cycles for its Windows and Office applications. As the world moved forward, with Google becoming dominant online and Apple owning the market for mobile products, Microsoft struggled to keep up. This was characterized by unevenly executed new products (e.g., Zune), in which even the company soon lost interest.

After being named CEO in February 2014, Satya Nadella undertook a major restructuring of the massive company to do away with the destructive internal competition. Products and platforms would no longer exist as separate groups; rather, all Microsoft employees would begin focusing on a limited set of common goals, including reinventing productivity and business processes, building the intelligent cloud platform, and creating more personal computing.

In September 2016, Nadella shook up the company again by merging the Microsoft Research Group with the Bing, Cortana, and Information Platform teams to create a new artificial intelligence and research group. With about 5,000 engineers and computer scientists, the new group's goal was artificial intelligence innovation across the Microsoft product line.

Microsoft's future does look brighter as a result of the still-ongoing reorganization, but perhaps its greatest achievement has already been realized: to offer employees a new sense that their work has real meaning.

Mergers—Sirius and XM

In July 2008, Sirius Satellite Radio joined forces with rival XM Satellite Radio. Megan Ruesink writes in a Rasmussen University blog that the merger was officially announced more than a year prior but was delayed due to one problem—when satellite radio first began in 1997, the FCC granted only two licenses, with the condition that neither of the holders would acquire control of the other.

So Sirius and XM filed the proper paperwork with the FCC, allowed the FCC to investigate the merger, and waited patiently for approval. Today, 70 percent of new cars come with a free three-month trial of SiriusXM satellite radio, and the new company's net income and revenue continue to increase.

Acquisitions that Create New Products or Services—du Telecom and Huawei Technologies

The United Arab Emirates' du Telecom provides mobile and fixed telephony, broadband connectivity, and internet protocol television to consumers and businesses. In 2006, the company began operating in a highly competitive market. By 2010, du Telecom had acquired almost 40 percent of the region's market share and was able to maintain a growth rate of over 32 percent.

But the company's leaders, according to Dora Wang, had no desire to rest on their laurels. In 2013, du Telecom signed a memorandum of understanding (MOU) to improve its project management capabilities with China's Huawei Technologies Company Limited, a multinational networking and telecommunications equipment and services provider.

Due to Huawei's connections to the Chinese government, the relationship was controversial. But since signing the MOU, du Telecom has achieved:

- Reductions in project failure and in the number of employees needed per project

- Lower costs, tighter time frames, and projects that cost less than predicted, thanks to a single point of contact who manages the project

Transformational Change

Transformational change, as defined by the Andersons, is brought on by market requirements that force fundamental changes in strategy, operations, and worldview. The new state is predicted. It emerges from visioning, trial and error, and discovery and requires a monumental shift in mindset, behavior, and culture. Everyone in the organization must operate from this framework in order for the change to be sustained.

Transformational change represents a radical shift in organizational focus structurally, strategically, and culturally. Therefore, it can produce fear, doubt, and insecurity. When making transformational changes, it is important to create and communicate a well-defined strategy and plan developed in concert with key stakeholders throughout the organization.

Given the enormity of transformational change, failure along the way is a possibility. If this happens, it may be necessary to examine the business processes that the change is anchored to and the goals that make the change actionable. It also may be advantageous to revert to the developmental and transitional levels at which the organization continuously learns from mistakes, adopts remedies, and improves incrementally, leading toward transformation.

Christopher Smith, in "Understanding Transformational Change Management," identifies several categories of transformation and highlights organizations that have successfully navigated each. Some examples follow.

Applying New Technology—Nokia

Nokia is one of the world's leading makers of cell phones, yet the company began in 1865 as a paper mill. Following World War II, Nokia entered the telegraph and telephone business as a cable manufacturer and was making televisions by the 1980s. Nokia transformed itself into a manufacturer of cell phones during the Finnish recession of the 1990s, when the company streamlined its business to stay profitable.

Restructuring Products—Apple

In 1996, Apple was losing money and had very little market share when it purchased former owner Steve Jobs' software company, NeXT. In 1997, Jobs again became CEO of Apple and began restructuring the product line, placing greater emphasis on style and proprietary hardware and ending its practice of licensing its operating system to other hardware manufacturers. The transformation to focus on quality and innovation led to a return to prosperity.

Repositioning Markets—McDonald's

In 2006, McDonald's suffered its first-ever quarterly loss and was under fire from anti-obesity and anti-junk food campaigners. Under direction from CEO John Skinner, McDonald's began transforming its culture, adding espresso drinks and healthier menu items and updating the look of its stores to focus on what its customers really wanted. By becoming more customer-focused, McDonald's built a culture of caring and empathy that brought it back into profit.

Operations Interrelated with Change—Nokia

Nokia, previously cited as an example of transformational change, is also an example of how operations and change are connected as an aspect of continuous improvement. As indicated earlier, the company started as a paper mill more than 150 years ago. However, it has found and nurtured success in a range of industrial sectors, including cable, paper products, rubber boots, tires, televisions, and mobile phones.

Nokia's journey to a telecommunications focus began in the 1990s. By 1998, the company became the best-selling mobile phone brand in the world. In 2011, to address increasing competition from Apple's iOS and Google's Android operating systems, Nokia entered into a strategic partnership with Microsoft and sold its mobile device business to that company. This action led to the creation of Nokia Networks following the purchase of joint-venture partner Siemens in 2013, which laid the foundation for Nokia's transformation into a network hardware and software provider.

Next, the purchase of telecommunications equipment provider Alcatel-Lucent, among other acquisitions, greatly broadened the scope of Nokia's portfolio and customer base. The company was now positioned to transition to fifth-generation (5G) wireless technology capable of connecting a wider range of devices to a network 100 times faster than current cellular networks and 10 times faster than the fastest home broadband service. According to Roger Cheng in the article "5G is Almost a Reality. Here's What It'll Really Feel Like," this speed, combined with responsiveness and reach, could unlock the full capabilities of technology to support self-driving cars, remote surgeries, drones, and virtual reality.

The acquisition of Alcatel-Lucent was particularly important because that company owned Bell Labs, which had an unparalleled history of technological innovation—including lasers, transistors, and UNIX, a widely known multi-user operating system. Bell Labs researchers led analog, digital, and mobile shifts in communication technology, the development of the Internet, and the innovation of wavelength division multiplexing, enabling huge increases in network capacity. The company pioneered the mobile revolution, from the first hand-held mobile phone in 1973 to the first calls on second-generation (2G) and fourth-generation (4G) wireless networks. Given Nokia's desire to become a world leader in the application of 5G technology, the purchase of Alcatel-Lucent and its affiliate Bell Labs (now Nokia Bell Labs) was a wise investment.

This acquisition demonstrates how Nokia applied transitional change to achieve continuing transformational change—positioning the company to create the infrastructure for 5G, which Nokia believes will shape the future of technology to transform the human experience and increase its ability to offer the only end-to-end network capability in this arena.

Even as Nokia seeks to operate more at the transitional and transformational change levels, it continues to benefit from a commitment to developmental change, especially in refocusing its marketing strategies and updating technology to support existing and prospective tasks. A great example of this is found in Nokia's "four pillars strategy," which is designed to prepare more of its customers, notably communication service providers, to be competitive in the 5G environment.

The first pillar, "leading in high-performance end-to-end networks," is designed to educate customers about the benefits of 5G over previous generations of technology.

The second pillar is "expanding network sales beyond current customers to select markets." By targeting web-based companies, extra-large enterprises that use technology as a competitive advantage, and large players in the transportation, energy, and public sectors (such as Amazon, Fujitsu, and Philips), Nokia's goal is to help prepare organizations to digitize their operations.

With the third pillar, "building a strong, standalone software business at scale," Nokia developed its first dedicated software sales force and acquired a business to enhance its software intelligence and automation capabilities.

Nokia expects to sell these capabilities to customers to improve the digital experience, implement innovative business models, and unlock new revenue opportunities.

The fourth pillar is "creating new business and licensing opportunities in the consumer ecosystem." In 2018, Nokia signed several new patent licensing agreements, developed licensing businesses in new sectors, including the automotive industry and locations such as China and India, and launched several Nokia-branded smartphones. These additional actions will eventually lead the 5G distribution market.

In summary, the types of change are all connected yet fluid. The organizations that reach the highest level—transformational change—do so only because they experience in some fashion the benefits of developmental and transitional change and ongoing improvement in business processes. For organizations that seek to remain viable, like Nokia, the focus on change within the context of normal operations is critical. In this regard, Deming suggests that organizations must have a deep and abiding dedication to constant, ongoing development—continuous improvement.

III. Foundations for Ongoing Change

"Standing still is the fastest way of moving backwards in a rapidly changing world."

– Lauren Bacall

Nokia is an example of how developmental, transitional, and transformational change work together for continuous improvement, implying that change is an integral component of regular operations. This idea counters the belief that change is sporadic, occurs occasionally, and is relegated to specific issues and areas of the organization. Again, some existing change models reinforce this notion. But smaller ongoing transformations, such as those that make business processes more efficient and effective, occur more often. It is within this context that change has the greatest potential to improve productivity and make organization-wide transformation more realistic. In *Awake at the Wheel: Moving Beyond Change Management to Conscious Change Leadership*, Linda Ackerman Anderson and Dean Anderson say that effective business processes dictate how change is carried out, contributing to the way that the organization discovers and accomplishes its business results while meeting its people and cultural requirements.

In effect, the type of change that leads to organizational transformation is anchored in ongoing process improvements. Andy Rowsell-Jones and John Roberts of the Gartner Group define this type of change as a disciplined approach to organizational development that improves performance, drives operational excellence, and leads to continuous improvement. Among the benefits of process improvement is increased efficiency through recognizing and eliminating duplication and other challenges. Once a process becomes more efficient, execution is enhanced, leading to greater effectiveness. Ultimately, organizations become more agile and respond more quickly to market demands triggered by such things as innovations in technology. Most importantly, employees become accustomed to change as a normal occurrence. In this way, process improvements can serve as a foundation for more ambitious change.

When business process development is an afterthought, an organization is invariably fraught with serious problems created by eroding the foundation of the change process. This erosion, according to the team at Planview.com, begins with customer complaints, poor product quality, frustrated employees, and wasted resources.

The PDCA Cycle

In "Process Improvement Projects On-Boarding & Off-Boarding," David McCoy suggests that there are two objectives for process improvement: to resolve a problem with an existing process or to introduce a new process. To assess when either is necessary, an organization should conduct a review in the context of continuous improvement and the PDCA format inspired by Deming. This approach is based on Deming's admonishment that meaningful improvement, especially when structured, process-oriented, and employee-centered, improves products, services, and employee satisfaction.

The PDCA Cycle, as outlined below, is divided into four phases that help leaders analyze and improve a single process. The cycle provides for continuous review until the process is performing well in response to the aims of the unit and organization.

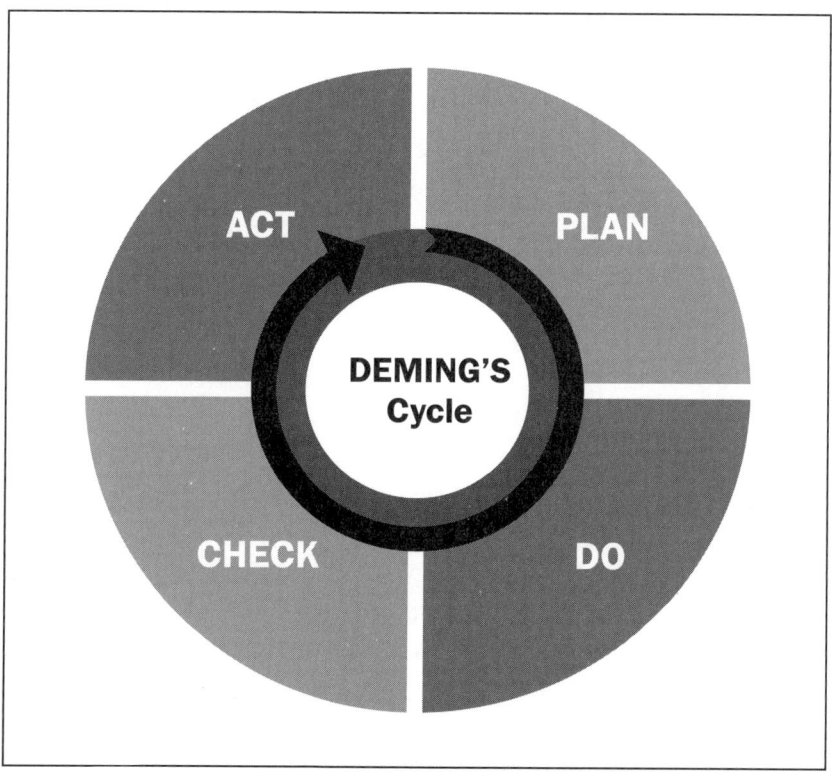

Plan

Before the improvement or introduction of a process, it is important to have some understanding of the current process, if any exists. An easy way to accomplish this is to create a flowchart that illustrates the steps in the process and how they are carried out. This action makes it easier to pinpoint more precisely the issue with the current process or what a replacement or an additional process needs to achieve.

As an example of how this works, we will turn once again to Nokia. This broad-scope telecommunications company headquartered in Finland boasts sales totaling $9.8 billion in 130 countries and 41,000 employees worldwide. Given the enormity of its operations, Nokia has invested significantly in developing business processes, including software development. Prior to 1997, there were no clearly defined processes in this area—an omission that quickly contributed to worsening performance and that became an urgent concern for the company. The telecommunications industry was advancing rapidly, and a downturn in the European economy, especially in Russia, added to the necessity to institute these improvements.

Nokia hired a consulting firm, ICL Limited, for its expertise in business analysis. The ICL consultants and a steering group—composed of senior management, representatives from the information management group, and employees from other business groups—mapped processes based on earlier Nokia descriptions, created technology tools to manage them, and identified facilitators to train end users throughout Nokia's vast employee base.

Do

Deming suggests that a process improvement should be implemented as a pilot until there is certainty that it works. He believes it's too risky to use the new process throughout the organization until it works better than the old.

To continue with the Nokia example, the company undertook a pilot project with the support of another vendor with expertise in information management. The consultants evaluated the initial processes for clarity and applicability, then divided the pilot project into four phases: starting point, process specifications and project plan, technology selection, and results. Accordingly, the process documents were completed, a technology toolkit to manage the processes was selected, and the pilot process provided the framework for future refinements.

Check

Leaders should evaluate improvements by determining if the revamped or new process is beneficial in both the short and long terms. If the process works, it can be scaled up, and the organization can move on to the final PDCA step: Act. If the results are inconclusive, the cycle should return to the previous step or to the beginning. This is why the PDCA approach is cyclical—to allow leaders to work in all dimensions at once to ensure that the process, whether existing or proposed, is working.

In concert with the Check phase of PDCA, Nokia revised the process descriptions three times during the pilot. The final document was completed alongside the development of a technology tool for managing the processes. Nokia experienced benefits from the exercise in three distinct areas: technical, business, and organizational.

In the technical area, milestones that acted as quality control and decision points were created for each process. This was possible because each process was graphically illustrated, making it easier for the end users to apply. Templates that prescribed inputs were supported by guidelines that conveyed how each activity should be performed. The technology tool supported the end user and allowed for easy analysis of the output in an electronic format.

Initially, the new processes proved beneficial in the business area for reducing original process times and simplifying the system structure. The success of the pilot phase and the availability of the initial drafts were important for achieving buy-in by the end users.

At the organizational level, the creation of the business processes led to the reorganization of the information management division. The new structure was divided between the technical and process dimensions of software. And to ensure the success of the changes, a new job was established to oversee process implementation, performance, and development.

Act

Once success has been achieved at the Check phase, characterized by evaluating the process's effectiveness, the process should be introduced organization-wide.

At Nokia, the software development process was scaled across the company. It led to the integration of process thinking with system development, which was the project's goal. The project also proved beneficial as a platform for other initiatives. Although Nokia was primarily interested in formulating its software development processes, the project teams expanded their view to other processes to help information management technicians develop their skills in mapping and building processes.

On a larger scale, according to Tero Lindholm, who studied Nokia's software improvement process, the company learned valuable lessons that will serve it steadfastly as it seeks to become a world leader in the application of 5G technology. During the project, Nokia found that:

- Communication is important to keeping the project alive.

- Management support and involvement is critical.

- The reasons for undertaking the project must be clear from the beginning.

- Clear milestones are necessary to move the project along.

- Quick wins must be achieved to demonstrate the possibilities.

- Business processes must be easy to understand, learn, and support.

- Funding is important for operations, consultants, technology, and training and practice for all end users.

As a follow-up on this program, Jaakko Aspara and his associates found that Nokia's software development process had broader implications. For example, the process raised awareness and understanding of business model innovations such as the mass-market opportunities associated with 5G technology. The experience gained by middle managers, combined with their technological capability, allowed for the consideration of practices different than those mandated at the corporate level while maintaining adherence to Nokia's strategic priorities. In other words, as a result of the software process improvements, business unit managers perceived important changes in markets and the business environment in general and offered concrete strategic alternatives. Finally, the authors note that a set of proven routines and capabilities is a necessary requirement for an evolving business environment—in this case technology—in which change is not only ongoing but also pervasive.

It is important to continue measuring effectiveness during the Act phase, as seen in the Nokia case. And, once again, if problems are encountered, the PDCA cycle allows for continued iterations until the process is optimized and perfected. As indicated in the more extensive illustration of the PDCA cycle below, the phases represent individual actions that not only overlap but also allow for reverting back to the previous phases to ensure that every conceivable aspect of formulating, piloting, and assessing the process has been considered.

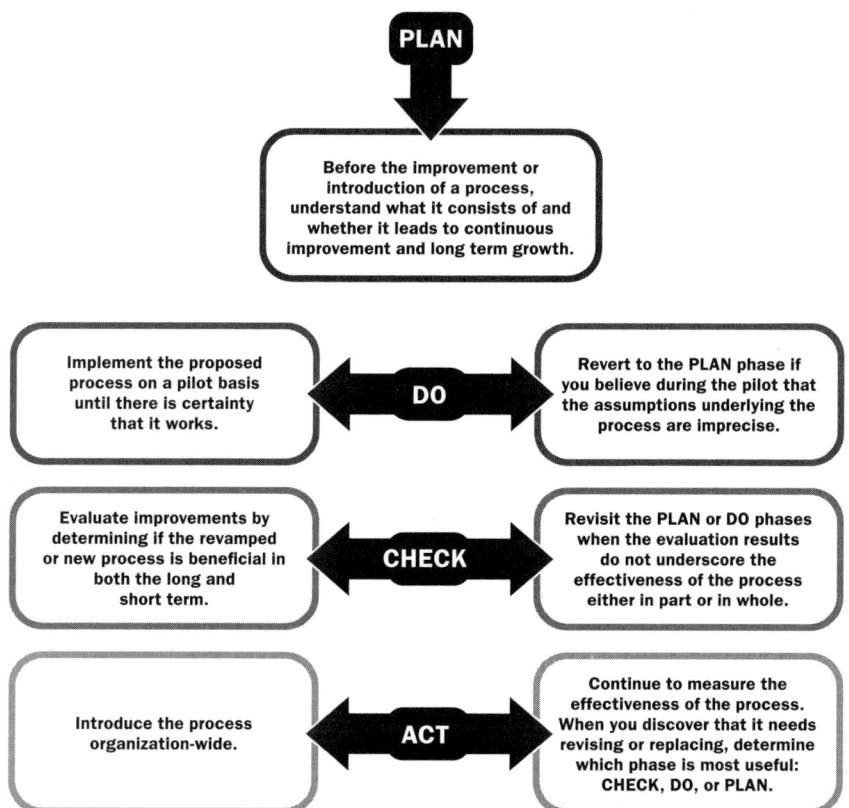

On this note, I offer a word of caution: Applying PDCA effectively can be intense and time-consuming. There *will* be repetition and overlap. It is important, therefore, to first establish the value of the process to the organization's advancement. If this value is confirmed, the cycle can be used to create a flowchart, identify appropriate remedies, implement the process on a localized basis, measure effectiveness in this environment, scale it throughout the organization, and continue monitoring it to ensure long-term viability.

The Gartner Group recommends a method for evaluating the effectiveness of the process through key performance indicators (KPIs) that depict the actionable milestones as measured at the organizational, individual, and change levels.

KPIs determine the effectiveness of the process at regular intervals and contribute incrementally to fulfilling organizational priorities. This is why the assessment process is critical not only in the Act phase but also throughout the other phases and beyond the PDCA cycle altogether. As improvements occur, leaders must monitor, evaluate, and build upon them to ensure that they are contributing to continuous improvement that supports movement toward loftier ambitions—in Nokia's case, to position the company as a leader in the 5G technology realm.

Concomitant Interfacing

As noted, change leading to continuous improvement and organizational transformation is anchored in dependable, up-to-date processes using the PDCA cycle. The recurring approach gives organizations the opportunity to work more efficiently, evaluate improvements at every phase, and ultimately accommodate more ambitious change. This interaction is important. Change is not just an ongoing aspect of operational improvement; all aspects of change are in fact interwoven.

I refer to this concept as concomitant interfacing, an idea that I adapted from medical science, in which the concomitant administration of two or more drugs is either the course of treatment or a means to counteract the possible side effects of a primary drug. The two or more interfacing drugs provide a balanced, necessary approach that ensures that the medicines work both individually and interdependently to reach a proposed state of wellness.

Similarly, viewing organizational change as concomitant interfacing emphasizes that all manner of change occurs simultaneously for good. This interfacing serves as the connector—very often technology—that links all the components together. This can be observed in the previously referenced Shell Oil Company example, with the interlinked process changes across the company's varied business units. Concomitant interfacing is vital for determining the status of initiatives and movement toward organizational advancement. This integration, when managed effectively and matched with an approach like UnCLE, discussed in the next chapter, contributes to continuous improvement.

Concomitant interfacing does this in two ways. First, it ensures that adequate foundations are in place in the form of structures and processes. These accommodate transformation at the organizational level and the attendant change in units, divisions, or departments. In these areas, business processes need to be re-engineered or behaviors modified to achieve the desired state.

Second, as noted in the illustration below, concomitant interfacing allows leaders to implement and handle the three types of change simultaneously:

- Developmental change, characterized by periodic improvements to enhance or correct certain aspects of the organization

- Transitional change encompassing the situational implementation of a desired new state different from the existing one

- Transformational change brought on by market conditions of more epic proportions that force fundamental changes in strategy, operations, and worldview

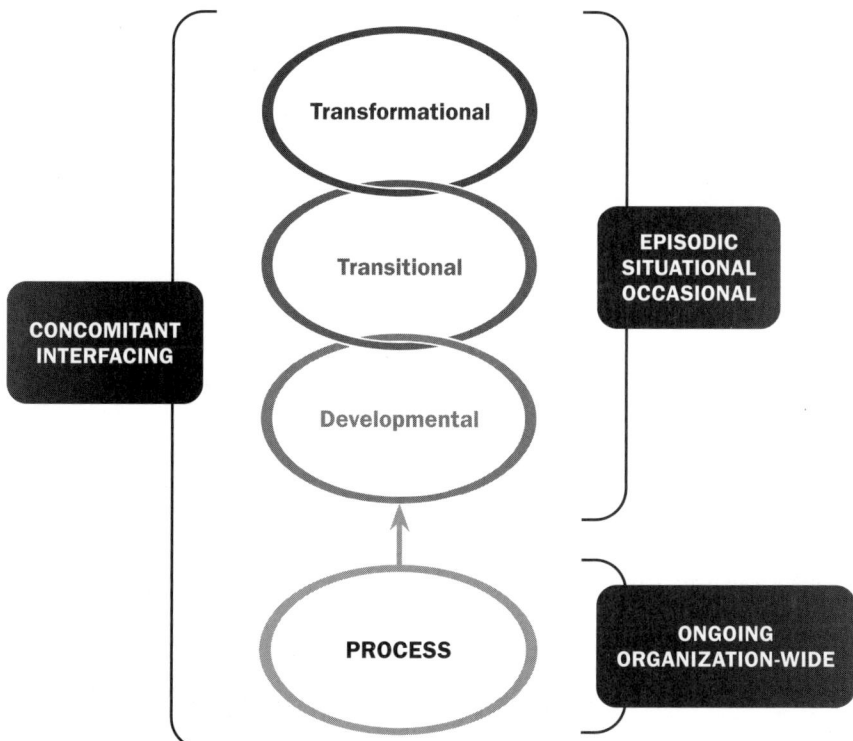

In order for concomitant interfacing to be useful in both of these ways, the strategic priorities of the organization must be clear. There must be actionable, measurable steps and goals for achieving these priorities, and leaders must understand their roles and responsibilities within this context.

An example of how concomitant interfacing might look is again found in Nokia. The company's vision is to become the primary conduit for businesses that want to thrive in the 5G technology realm. Nokia realized that to achieve this lofty position, it needed to improve business processes for software development, institute the four pillars strategy mentioned earlier, and secure acquisitions through which elements of the acquired businesses could be used to improve its position. All of these movements encompass the three types of change buttressed by business process development and a technology linchpin—hence, concomitant interfacing.

To benefit from concomitant interfacing, leaders must recognize where their organizations are situated with respect to change. This analysis permits leading organizational improvement in a gradual and calculated manner. However, it must be built on a foundation of understanding the different types of change, pinpointing through benchmarks (i.e., KPIs) where each type is occurring, and determining their collective impact on the organization as it travels the road to transformation. That journey, by the way, has no destination—only way stations at which new challenges are introduced and designed to take the organization to new heights.

In conclusion, I believe that continuous improvement is deeply rooted in organizational advancement, which includes change as an important element of that advancement. The wisdom of this approach has been seen at Nokia, a longstanding and self-regarding organization whose transformation has been deliberate yet positioned to respond to urgency. A system is now in place at the company through which developmental, transitional, and transformational change interconnect, as in concomitant interfacing, with strong and adaptable business processes that adhere to PDCA principles. All elements need to be in play to promote change within the context of normal operations, leading to organizational excellence.

Remember, the process is a cycle. If the test fails, return to the beginning and try again. If it works, monitor results and start again with a new plan to promote additional improvements.

The work of continuous improvement is never-ending.

IV. The Uninterrupted Cycle of Leadership Effectiveness (UnCLE)

*"The greatest danger in times of turbulence is not the turbulence—
it is to act with yesterday's logic."*

– Peter Drucker

In the preceding chapters, I have shown how change can harm organizations when issues that drive it go unchecked or, conversely, how change can be captured to promote advancement and growth. The latter occurs when the foundations of the organization—vision and strategy—are in place. Also evident is the realization that change is progressive, iterative, and overlapping. In addition, there are methods for improving and replacing business processes through the PDCA cycle, which is the foundation for ongoing operations involving change.

The process of concomitant interfacing occurs over time, across and deeply within the organization; it requires the involvement of everyone. Therefore, understanding concomitant interfacing is among the first steps toward becoming a more astute leader of change. Such a leader, with the ability to anticipate trends, is equipped to respond proactively to drivers of change, is committed to consistency of purpose, and is dedicated to constant improvement in a systematic fashion.

Change management systems are not equipped to serve in support of this holistic approach, nor are they adequate for responding to the multifaceted ways that change can present itself. So leaders must apply a method that allows for continuous improvement as an ongoing process, not a momentary or occasional effort. Real success comes when continuous improvement becomes business as usual.

A blog post by the company Kanbanize underscores this notion by describing effective implementation of continuous improvement:

> *It's not finding a method that works and sticking with it. It's looking at where you are today, setting a goal, and doing what needs to be done to reach that goal. Once that goal is met, you start again, finding ways to improve further. It doesn't matter what kind of industry or business you're in—a continuous improvement approach is necessary to keep ahead of the game. Continuous improvement can range from simple changes in the day-to-day workings of your company to major shifts in focus and procedures across a global structure.*

This is no easy task. Continuous improvement cannot be carried out haphazardly or isolated from the work that people perform every day. Thus, a system must be installed that makes change initiatives a priority within ongoing operations. This "system" connotes the salient processes that are easily understood by everyone and that create ways for individuals to implement change and to be consulted about the implications of change in their areas of responsibility.

At the same time, according to Ron Ashkenas in "It's Time to Rethink Continuous Improvement," disruption is necessary to encourage creativity, and the system of change must embrace this. When required, the organizational framework should be realigned to accommodate the system of change. And when possible and when there is a sense of urgency, change should be accelerated through piloting at scale. Finally, this system must contain mechanisms for evaluating the effectiveness of the effort and for celebrating success.

This is where my UnCLE system is advantageous. As introduced in *Change the Lapel Pin*, UnCLE is an agent of continuous improvement. It helps to reliably obtain desired outcomes that, when built upon, generate repeated success and organizational excellence. It incorporates change into the fabric of the organization as opposed to focusing on it peripherally.

The process begins with recognizing "causes for action"—trends and predicaments that might be disruptive to an organization or, even more importantly, opportunities to build upon existing initiatives. Next, UnCLE helps identify the short- and long-term solutions to address the cause for action and then measures the outcomes to determine if the remedies are effective. Finally, UnCLE permits building upon and celebrating these outcomes to sustain change as another cause for action rises to the fore.

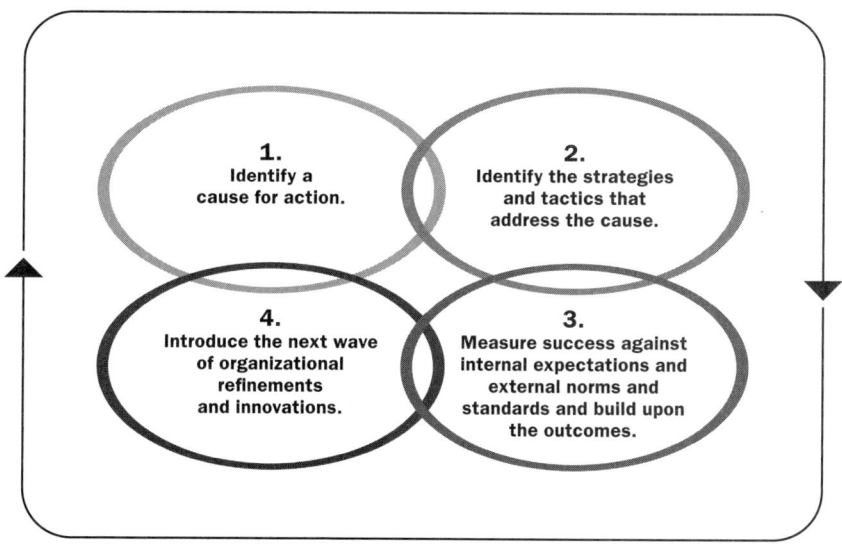

While including PDCA's focus on business processes, UnCLE provides a more robust framework to improve operations and accommodate ongoing change. The structure of UnCLE allows for these transactions because the elements are cyclical rather than linear, interrelated as opposed to independent, and recurring instead of static. It is a fluid and interdependent approach to change that can be applied across the organization at all levels. The elements are not starting and ending points, but rather intersections at which leaders seek clarity on where the organization is and where it needs to go to achieve predetermined outcomes.

These are fundamental components of continuous improvement. Applied though UnCLE, continuous improvement becomes a multidimensional process rather than sudden, unplanned, boundless change. UnCLE calls for clear actions with achievable targets and measurements for success as well as continuous alignment of both organizational framework and culture. This kind of precise coordination of change in the context of operations is a mainstay of continuous improvement.

In the UnCLE system, individuals anticipate and respond to change more easily because they are accustomed to it. They have heard the narrative and have experienced the results that convince them that change is necessary. They often look forward to the process and outcomes because of the rewards both professionally and personally.

UnCLE does this, in part, through the concept of appreciative inquiry (AI), which was pioneered in the 1980s by David Cooperrider and Suresh Srivastva, two professors at the Weatherhead School of Management at Case Western Reserve University. AI promotes collaborative and strengths-based change by questioning the current status and future of an organization. It helps systems like UnCLE facilitate positive change in organizations, groups, and communities. Its assumption, according to the Center for Appreciative Inquiry, is simple: All systems have something that works right—something that gives them life when they are vital, effective, and successful. AI is enacted, in part, through questions (like those associated with each element of UnCLE) that identify positive components and connect them to heighten energy, sharpen vision, and inspire action for change.

Jacqueline Stavros and Cheri Torres, in their book *Conversations Worth Having: Using Appreciative Inquiry to Fuel Productive and Meaningful Engagement*, contend that AI focuses on strategic organizational development by looking at assets, including the leader and people and the strengths-filled, opportunity-rich world around them. They note that this is not so much a shift in the methods and models of organizational operations involving change but a fundamental shift in how an organization gets to what is important through inquiry into what constitutes the organization's strengths, possibilities, and successes.

With respect to AI and UnCLE, the assumption is that everyone is involved regularly in the ongoing process of examining and questioning. This includes discerning the impact of existing and proposed actions and how the information and data derived from their application is applied to foster ongoing change. Therefore, dealing with change is viewed as a shared responsibility, based on in-depth analysis using AI, to bring insight and direction at every juncture of UnCLE.

Let's look at this process through an application of each element of UnCLE and how the associated AI questions are addressed. In *Change the Lapel Pin*, I presented an example of how I applied UnCLE to promote positive change in graduation rates and other student success metrics early in my presidency at Cuyahoga Community College in Cleveland, Ohio. However, this improvement was not an isolated change. The manner in which this initial change became incorporated into the culture of the institution as a system for continuous improvement serves as an example of how UnCLE and AI may be used in tandem to promote ongoing operations and change.

Identify a Cause for Action

Given UnCLE's definition of a cause for action, the AI questions that seem plausible within this element are:

- What trends will disrupt our business?

- What impact will they have on our organization? What do the data indicate?

- How should we respond?

- What outcomes do you expect?

Most change management systems ask leaders to identify a reason to change. John Kotter, author of *Leading Change* and creator of the very popular Eight-Step Process for Leading Change, calls this a sense of urgency that alerts the organization that change must occur and why. Jeff Hiatt, developer of the ADKAR model, refers to this step as "awareness of the need to change" in his book *Change Management: The People Side of Change*. However, these and other change management systems often assume that the identification of a reason to change is a monumental act at the province of the leader, who announces it and then communicates this decision to the individuals who must implement it. This act by the leader, because it discounts employee input, is among the primary reasons that change initiatives are met with resistance, according to Jiseon Shin et al. in *The Journal of Applied Behavioral Science*.

The reality is that many businesses are quick to recognize great ideas, but they often have no clue how to successfully integrate them into their business model. According to a blog post by Mike Myatt, a flawed execution can cast doubt on management credibility, have a negative impact on morale, and cause a variety of other problems for the organization, resulting in another change initiative that ends in frustration and wasted time and energy.

This is why addressing the AI questions is so very important: It assists in forming a solid base of evidence to substantiate the cause for action. A simple way to accomplish this is to recognize trends that are derived from research to expand understanding of the organization's current state and the external realities that underlie it. Reading reports from the broader industry, conferring with industry leaders, and consulting with individuals inside and outside the organization, including customers, can both confirm and instruct the approach. John Hall, writing for Inc., reinforces these actions by suggesting that they allow moving beyond conjecture and disorderly reasoning to recognizing and embracing trends that foretell what developments are around the corner and then evolving the strategic priorities to address them.

This approach boils down to three points made by McKinsey & Company in the report "Building Organizational Capabilities":

- Rely on a regimented approach for diagnosing problems rather than guesswork.

- Insist on data as background for decision-making rather than assumptions.

- Use simple statistical tools to organize data and draw inferences.

Next, the AI questions permit rapid identification of different tools and metrics for measuring the impact of the cause for action. This seems counterintuitive since it can appear to be an attempt to anticipate outcomes before establishing remedies. However, this action, tantamount to working backward, is an important first step in forming congruence among all elements of UnCLE.

There is a possibility that additional AI questions emanate from this exercise. Do not worry. This can be a very good thing, a sign that the organization is investing in validating the cause for action, which only leads to greater precision in responses to AI questions associated with the other elements.

Finally, answering the AI questions at this juncture ensures connection to the next element of UnCLE, which is focused on identifying the strategies and tactics in response to the cause for action. Once again, this is an opportunity to reinforce and assess the organization's preparation. Furthermore, it can ensure that the cause for action aligns with overall vision and mission and that it is not a disparate action but one that integrates with, builds upon, and adds value to existing initiatives.

The foregoing discussion supports why the term "identify a cause for action" in the UnCLE system differs from change management approaches in several distinct ways. First, it is predominantly an extension of an existing focus that is anchored by continually refined business processes— a staple of continuous improvement. Next, there is recognition of where the organization is positioned relative to the three types of change: developmental, transitional, and transformational. It is positioned in a solid and successful strategic plan. And, finally, it assumes that this state has been achieved, due in part to engagement by individuals throughout the organization. Some ways to accomplish this step are:

- Sharing data to demonstrate the importance of the initiative and how it builds upon existing efforts

- Taking seriously the recommendations from end users prior to implementation

- Ensuring that organizational decisions and proposed actions are aligned

- Requiring managers to talk directly and regularly with suppliers, customers, and other stakeholders

- Keeping the organization and other interested parties updated on progress

As described in *Change the Lapel Pin*, I and my colleagues at Tri-C responded to the requirement to increase degree attainment with a focus on improving students' access to the college and their success in a learner-centered environment characterized by superior programs and services. This is essentially our vision for the future, undergirded by the strategic areas I will expand upon later.

This presidency, my fourth, arrived at a challenging time in our nation's history. At that moment, the educational attainment of Americans 25 to 34 years old was ranked 16th among developing countries, and Ohio placed 39th among the 50 states in degree attainment. In Cleveland, the skills gap meant that only about 67 percent of available workers could compete for high-wage, high-tech jobs. And the rate at which our students attained credentials was unsatisfactory for an institution of our size and stature. This environment became our initial cause for action in accordance with the first element of UnCLE.

As the president, I recognized immediately that I would have to respond to this new form of "a nation at risk" to get individuals the degrees and certificates they sought in a timely manner and then guide them toward meaningful careers or to four-year institutions. We arrived at this "cause for action" based on a thorough analysis of evidence derived from data on student outcomes, including test scores and grades. We then asked more questions: What are the causes of student performance? What are the most promising interventions, following extensive conversations with all stakeholders? How do we implement the interventions—as pilots or immediately to scale? How do we know we have been successful? At some point, will we be able to predict educational attainment based on an analysis of the performance of individual students? We termed this approach Evidence, Inquiry, and Analytics.

Change is necessary for survival. This blunt declaration reflects what organizations must do to advance in a global market. Deciding on the specifics of change is tough, even when it is an outgrowth of the strategic direction of the organization. For this reason, leaders should always focus attention on systematic organizational development involving change to remain on a steady course to success, even and especially in the face of challenges.

Organizations equipped to respond to any eventuality are the ones that will advance. This entails not only recognizing trends and their impact but also how the organization should respond. This is why the first element of UnCLE is so critical: It allows for incorporating change using the all-important AI questions as starting points. These questions can be built upon to develop more deeply intrusive questions that actually test the assumptions and processes on which change is built. For example, in examining business processes, what is required to accommodate disruption: rebuilding, modifying, or eliminating elements? Does the organization's strategy support impending change? And what does this change mean to the people in the organization? Of course, there are actions that coincide with these deliberations, like reviewing available reports and data, especially those that inform decision-making. In all phases, communicating and consulting with the people who do the work is important. To echo the sentiments of Martin Zwilling in "6 Management Changes that will Transform Your Business Culture," stalwart organizations make and measure change as part of their normal strategies rather than focusing on it when a crisis occurs. They thrive on disruption, rather than fight and fear it.

Identify the Strategies and Tactics that Address the Cause for Action

Important AI questions that are associated with this element of UnCLE are:

- What are the short- and long-term strategies to address the sense of urgency?

- Do they flow from and enhance existing priorities and aims?

- Do they reflect national best practices and innovations developed and applied at our organization?

- Are they actionable and measurable?

Knowing why to change is the most important element of UnCLE since building change on unsubstantiated need can derail any effort. This second element, identifying strategies and tactics, is next in line of importance.

Some change management systems would view this phase as an opportunity to introduce a plan for change, like the McKinsey 7S framework. Sometimes these plans are essentially disconnected with the mission and vision of the organization and its strategic priorities and actions.

The UnCLE system assumes that a strategic plan is already in place to provide direction and purpose. The plan is accompanied by tactics designed to make actionable the agreed-upon priorities of the organization. These priorities—or pillars, as in Nokia's designation—are characterized as follows:

- They are clear, actionable, measurable steps and goals.

- The processes that undergird them as foundations are refined and replaced as needed.

- The priorities build upon the existing foundation and provide a platform for the next cause for action.

- Leaders understand their roles and responsibilities within this context.

The difference between change management and continuous improvement is discernible here—and the AI questions associated with this element of UnCLE address that difference. The answers to these questions can connect the cause for action to the all-important strategic plan and its short- and long-term goals.

Why is this important? Goals are a commitment to pursuing transformation and gaining a competitive advantage. Further, goals are actions that enable leaders to determine what is effective, to make corrections where necessary, and to measure and build upon growth and progress in support of the strategic plan and cause for action. The most important thing here is that the cause for action, the strategic plan, and the goals complement one another as they build upon current initiatives inside the organization. It is also important to look outside for benchmarks and promising practices that benefit the cause.

Further, goals need to be measurable—an aspect that is important to this element of UnCLE and essential to the next two. How does this happen? There are a number of possibilities, but I have found that KPIs compare performance across time to measure what has changed and to establish a basis for analysis. When undertaking this comparison, it is important to conduct research on competitors to determine how they are addressing similar initiatives. KPIs relate strategy to action, can be applied across units, and, importantly, are quantifiable. They also help highlight potential problems or opportunities and allow corrective actions as the cause for action is addressed.

As a demonstration of this process, I again draw on my work at Tri-C. The focus on improving educational attainment (termed Success and Completion) required us to transform the institution by identifying overall priorities, reframing the college, and implementing specific campus-based and college-wide actions. We established six strategic priorities:

- Creating a holistic student experience with more extracurricular activities

- Establishing more short-term workforce education programs

- Keeping tuition affordable

- Reducing the achievement gap experienced by minority, older, and low-income students

- Building on partnerships with the community

- Enriching the brand and image of the college

The interrelationship among these priorities is illustrated in the following chart.

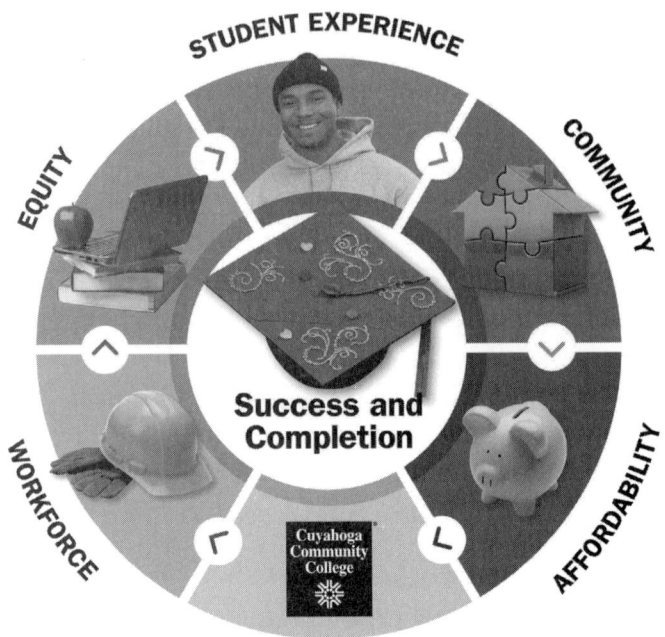

These strategic priorities required me to be intimately involved as a manager in developing and implementing the actions to meet these lofty and ambitious goals. This is the area in which leadership and management combine. I surmised that rather than a "top-down" or "bottom-up" philosophy to organizational development, my ambitions required collaborations, decisions, and work to be carried out on middle ground.

To accommodate the approach, I had to flatten a particularly hierarchical organizational structure to reflect one that ensured greater connection and communication at a micro level. I began this effort during my first year at the institution by expanding leadership groups to include a larger number of administrative leaders. Among these were my President's Cabinet (senior administrative leadership) and College-wide Cabinet, a large group consisting of middle management and above from across the college's four campuses and central administrative departments.

Even more critical was involving faculty leadership to a much greater degree through what became known as the President's Council, which was composed of the President's Cabinet, the Joint Faculty Senate Council, and faculty union leaders. A monthly gathering of this group became a forum for discussing key priorities at the college and brainstorming ways to collaboratively meet challenges. This group has been responsible for designing many pilot initiatives and identifying successful pilots that could be scaled across the institution.

I positioned the annual President's Renewal event as one of the keystone moments in our annual planning cycle. With participation by the President's Council and College-wide Cabinet, this event provides an opportunity to reflect on advancements toward the goals of the past year, to learn from business and educational thought leaders, to identify priorities for the coming year, and to actively begin the process of developing campus, divisional, or departmental goals to align with those priorities.

During the fall of 2014, under the banner "One Door, Many Options for Success," open working sessions at each campus helped employees at all levels to understand the six strategic priorities for student success and completion and to identify departmental and individual goals, processes, and initiatives to support them. Some of these initiatives were new; others were already in progress. The One Door framework provided a mechanism for connecting all of them to the priorities of the institution. As a result, every department and employee were invited to reconsider responsibilities and operations in light of the emphasis on student success. This gave the institution a common language and purpose, promoting a greater sense of unity.

The success of this element of UnCLE is an important milestone. It means that the counsel of stakeholders—who are trusted to carry out implementation and called upon to help determine both the scope and extent of change—has been heeded. Capitalizing on these interactions promotes commitment and success and develops champions who serve as models for even those who most ardently resist change. This leads to another important point: taking time to identify what might go wrong by anticipating potential barriers and devising mitigation strategies at the beginning of the initiative as well as throughout.

This element of UnCLE also requires communication to promote understanding and to demonstrate how change builds upon the foundation of the organization. Throughout this period, leaders must examine the impact on processes, work, and strategy. Without this examination, the change likely will not be sustained, and the organization can experience slippage.

Measure Success against Internal Expectations and External Norms and Standards

In exploring this element of UnCLE, appropriate AI questions are:

- How do we measure success for the strategies and tactics?

- Do the outcomes support them?

- Can we celebrate and build upon the results to improve organizational capacity?

- What do the outcomes suggest in determining next steps?

Most change management systems incorporate a stage or phase in which the impact of the change is measured. Often, the evaluation is focused on a single change initiative as opposed to change emanating from and leading to ongoing progress. In the case of UnCLE, the latter is the focus. Evaluation not only assesses the current state of the organization but also provides direction toward what might be next on the horizon.

It is important to ensure that the goals and KPIs established in the preceding element of UnCLE are both accurate and implementable. Why? Because evaluation builds upon them. These elements specify the key actions and anticipated outcomes in response to the cause for action; consequently, they must be substantiated through the evaluation process. Doing so helps identify assessment tools with greater precision.

This aspect of UnCLE truly defines the manner in which evaluation is carried out. It is an extensive and often tedious process—but it is necessary to measure the effectiveness of actions that address the cause for action and as a foundation for current and future initiatives. This is an important component of UnCLE because it supports deliberate and gradual transformation, a mainstay of continuous improvement. Let's take a look at how the AI questions help accomplish this objective by looking at some potential areas to measure.

First, finding and retaining customers is a crucial responsibility of any organization. So securing feedback from clientele, measuring their satisfaction, and gathering consumers' suggestions about what needs to be improved is an important way to determine the effectiveness of an organization's goals and KPIs.

Second, evaluating the performance of people, both individually and collectively, is necessary to determine their contributions, to clarify their roles in the process, and to make personnel adjustments where necessary. Also, measures of individuals' performance and behavior reveal if there is progress within units of change. This progress can be a determinant of overall success.

And, finally, at the organizational level, assessment considers many factors. It determines the extent that business operations and processes, such as those in finance and human resources, are effective. It evaluates the collective performance of all areas of the organization, including administrative, workforce, and customer-related functions. And lastly, it compares achievement against comparable organizations to identify competitive advantage and, most importantly, to help pinpoint next steps or subsequent causes for action. Here, leaders gain a more extensive understanding of how change efforts are progressing throughout an organization. This approach prepares them to demonstrate the effectiveness of actions and allows for identifying and fixing issues earlier in the transformation process to increase the chances of success.

In the case of Tri-C, each administrative area established benchmarks based on a model derived from the *Cleveland Clinic Way*, a book written by the clinic's former President and CEO, Dr. Delos "Toby" Cosgrove. In this model, Cosgrove presents a system based on national standards and best practice. It rates services that patients identify as important to them, measures the effectiveness of day-to-day operations, and determines the extent of the clinic's compliance with various regulatory agencies.

The benchmarks at Tri-C are extensive, but the most critical are those that measure our progress against vanguard colleges, such as recipients of the Aspen Prize, the Awards of Excellence from the American Association of Community Colleges, and the Leah Meyer Austen Award from Achieving the Dream. These include graduation rates and numbers, student return rates from one semester to the next, and pass rates in college-level mathematics and English. They are benchmarks that most effectively depict our progress against college strategic priorities and local and national norms.

When applying UnCLE, the momentum that accrues from improved outcomes becomes an excellent opportunity to determine if the benchmarks continue to be appropriate and whether the targets promote long-term improvements. In cases where targets are surpassed repeatedly, do not increase the target; this can seem like the rules are being changed in midstream after they have been agreed upon. Instead, introduce alongside the targets a series of stretch goals that may serve as motivation for increased action and commitment. Similarly, when targets are not attained, do not immediately change them. Rather, review the models on which they are based and assess the assumptions underlying them to determine if they continue to be appropriate and effective.

Thanks to the hard work and commitment of individuals across the organization, Tri-C quickly exceeded targets for many of the 51 performance measures that were aligned with the six strategic priorities. For example, beginning with the baseline year of 2010 and ending in 2020, we witnessed increases of more than 50 percent in the number of graduates completing degrees and certificates and more than 400 percent in the rate at which they completed these credentials. The following charts illustrate these important outcomes.

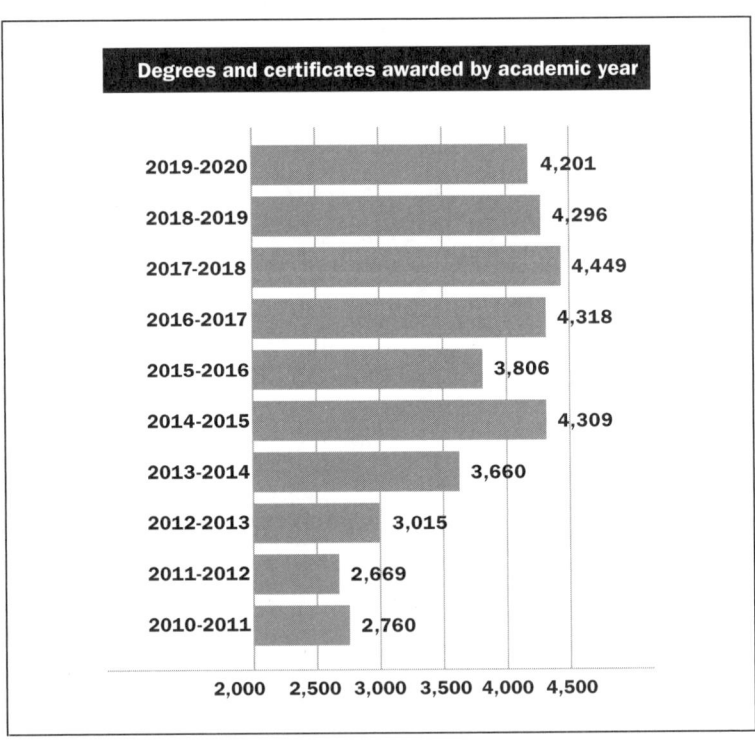

Degrees and certificates awarded by academic year

Academic Year	Count
2019-2020	4,201
2018-2019	4,296
2017-2018	4,449
2016-2017	4,318
2015-2016	3,806
2014-2015	4,309
2013-2014	3,660
2012-2013	3,015
2011-2012	2,669
2010-2011	2,760

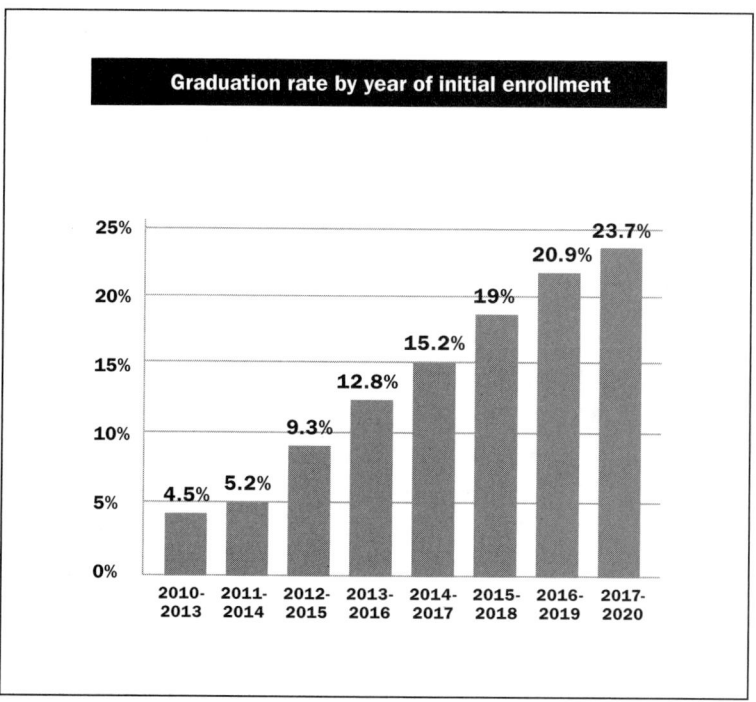

According to the magazine *Community College Times*, these accomplishments place our institution among the top tier of the nation's 1,108 community colleges. At the same time, students continue their education at increased levels and exhibit improved success in mathematics and English courses that serve as so-called "gateways" to degrees and certificates.

In recognition of these achievements and the college's overarching success, Tri-C received the prestigious Bellwether Award from the Community College Futures Assembly for achievements in workforce development programming. Its commitment to veterans and their families was recognized by the Kisco Foundation with the Kohlberg Prize, which included a cash award to offset the cost of a new veteran's center. For the first time in its decade-long association with Achieving the Dream (ATD), whose goal is to improve educational outcomes for minority students, the college qualified for the organization's prestigious Leah Meyer Austin Award. It was recognized as the ATD Leader College of Distinction and one of the nation's top community colleges by the Aspen Institute College Excellence Program's Top 150. And the Greater Cleveland Partnership, the city's economic development organization, recognized Tri-C for a third time as "Best in Class" for its commitment to a diverse workforce.

These were moments to celebrate the college's achievements and to think about how we could use that momentum to take the institution to even greater heights. Acknowledging and celebrating success is an important component of both change management and continuous improvement models. For example, number six of John Kotter's eight steps is to "create short term wins." According to Kotter, these wins are evidence of results that must be recognized and communicated early and often to track progress and energize employees. In the ADKAR approach, reinforcement ensures that change is sustained through rewards and recognitions and, conversely, corrective actions.

Celebrating milestones is an important aspect of UnCLE as well, especially in recognizing the benefits of continuous improvement. First, acknowledging milestones can provide valuable feedback on what is working and what might need changing. Next, celebrating is good for recognizing that accomplishments can be built from existing foundations, thus leading to transformation. Finally, acts of appreciation keep people motivated when they experience the benefits of continuous improvement to drive change.

In addition, according to Bill Carmody on *Inc.com*, celebrating reinforces the behavior that leaders want to see when a new challenge or opportunity emerges. So as accomplishments are recounted, skilled leaders will emphasize progress toward transforming systems, sparking new ideas and opportunities that build upon outcomes and assist in determining next steps.

This does not happen only during this element of UnCLE; feedback and reinforcement are necessary throughout. Frequent communication to provide updates, report on incremental success, and acknowledge involvement and commitment is also important. All of this helps to sustain change and position the organization for ongoing change and transformation.

Introduce the Next Wave of Organizational Refinements and Innovations

Several AI questions should be addressed in this element of UnCLE:

- Is our approach productive?

- Can we implement and sustain the outcomes?

- What is the next iteration of our response to the current or emerging cause for action?

Change management systems focus only on independent initiatives, not ones drawn from existing strategic priorities. And only one, John Kotter's approach, alludes to the importance of building upon and anchoring change experienced from these priorities.

Here is where continuous improvement most differs from and surpasses change management. Continuous improvement is constantly asking, "What happens when outcomes are achieved?" The response is to capitalize on the momentum to introduce continuing strategies and tactics that build upon the current iterations and frame the benchmarks and performance targets around them, just as the organization did previously.

When considering this aspect of continuous improvement, keep in mind that progress is almost never linear. Expect overlap, particularly when strategic priorities are multiple. Setbacks are a possibility, so it is important to periodically review progress to guard against stasis.
On occasion, it may be necessary to eliminate or modify existing strategies or to introduce new ones if the current path proves ineffectual. This understanding is important to ensure that outcomes lead to the next level of transformation.

At this point, and in accordance with the AI questions, it is necessary to survey all actions and processes to ensure that they are congruent and address together the cause for action. This is an important step to determine the extent of transformation and to build organizational capacity for ongoing continuous improvement.

In a *Harvard Business Review* article, David Garvin writes that beneath this effort is a commitment to learning. Leaders must implement actions that assimilate learning to sustain results and transform the culture. This learning is part of an infrastructure for managing and integrating continuous improvement, including a commitment to the cause for action, compliance with strategic objectives, risk mitigation, and evaluation. As James Harrington and his co-authors suggest in "Model for Sustainable Change," knowledge of how to carry out continuous improvement is important since the life cycle of transformation can last for years. Transitions are bound to occur, and in the absence of this learning framework, organizations and individuals can revert to past behaviors. Change remains cosmetic, and improvements are short-lived.

At Tri-C, the One Door framework became this infrastructure for ongoing innovation. "One Door, Many Options for Success" originally referred to the experience of incoming students: They would be able to enter the institution by any office or program and receive the same quality and scope of service directing them toward and along their best educational pathway. This was an ambitious goal for an institution serving more than 50,000 students annually through 190 career and technical programs across four campuses and several educational centers, each with a unique student demographic and distinct culture—but as already noted, the initiative has led to notable gains in performance measures related to student success.

However, it quickly became evident that the *process* of the One Door initiative was far more flexible than we had initially realized; as important as the results were to the college, the One Door framework itself was possibly even more valuable. The process effectively garnered feedback and involvement from every corner of the institution—and beyond. It instilled a common language and talking points in employees of widely differing responsibilities and levels of contact with students. And it provided college-wide impetus for change in a way that inspired the creation of new initiatives while naturally incorporating existing programs and promoting continuous improvement in processes to benefit the student experience. Thus, One Door came to refer less to an isolated initiative and more to a process. It came to refer not to a door entered by incoming students but to a common gateway to transformation at the college.

The flexibility of the One Door model became evident in the summer of 2015, when we celebrated the progress made during the year-long emphasis on student success. Yet even as we marked our achievements, we realized that not all students were seeing equal gains. As a result, while maintaining progress toward our overall student success goals, we embarked on a parallel and very similar process—this time with a focus specifically on equity in outcomes.

A college-wide equity summit and listening sessions on the campuses led to the creation of a college-wide tactical plan for equity. Again, beginning with the annual President's Renewal, each division, campus, and department was tasked with identifying measurable goals to support equity in outcomes for our students. An equity goal became a required component of the employee evaluation process. As a result, we have seen ongoing progress toward our equity priorities. In fact, equity is no longer a separate strategic priority but is embedded in every conceivable activity of the college along with access and success. The updated figure below demonstrates this change.

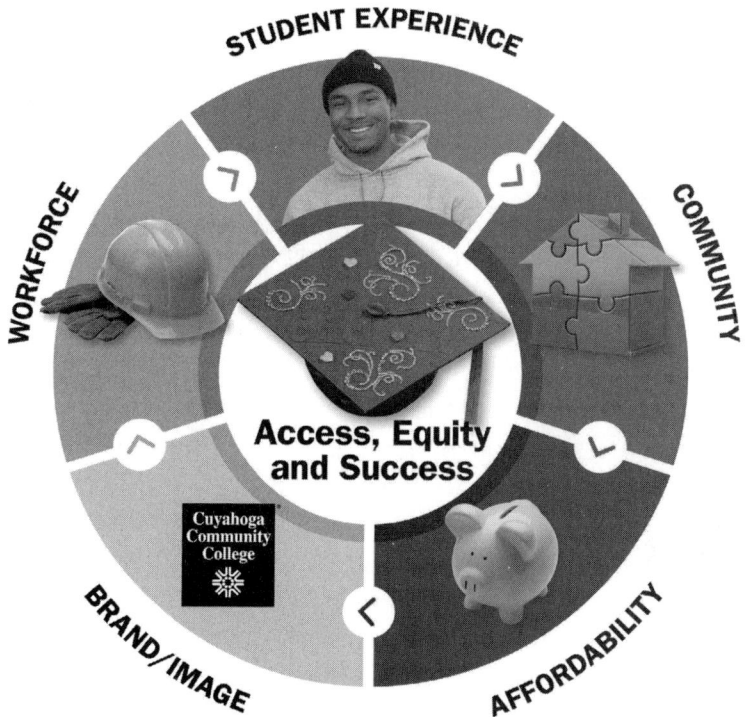

As a new college strategic planning cycle began in 2017, we immediately reached for the One Door framework. Now familiar to most employees at the institution, the title was becoming shorthand for a collaborative, inclusive process to address top priorities of the college. Again, strategic plan listening and work sessions were hosted across the college. There was at least one session at every campus and administrative facility, along with sessions and surveys designed specifically for participation by students as well as community partners and leaders. These sessions provided opportunities for employees, students, and community stakeholders to shape and refine actions and goals that were built on the foundational principles of the institution, including the mission, vision, and values. In the end, more than 1,800 individuals participated in the process of developing the strategic plan, Building Excellence through Access, Equity, and Success, which contributed to a greater sense of ownership in this guiding document for the institution.

Beginning in 2018, a renewed focus on college access became the latest initiative to apply the One Door framework. Initial efforts at the annual President's Renewal led to inclusive sessions at each campus involving administrators, faculty, and staff from all areas of the college. The President's Council and College-wide Cabinet continued to support and guide the work as divisions, campuses, departments, and employees set goals and established or strengthened processes to contribute to the effort. Any employee could receive training to become an Access Champion (an individual who would work directly with K–12 students and other community members in their recruitment and matriculation to the college). Several new access centers were created in coordination with community partner organizations in strategic neighborhoods throughout the community. These centers help support incoming students and provide points of contact between the community and the college and its programs. Our community partners and other groups staff access center advisory boards that help plan programming and next steps for the centers.

The college has experienced remarkable progress within the UnCLE framework, as demonstrated by outcomes portrayed in the charts shown previously. Through the AI and iterative growth model embodied by the UnCLE framework, One Door has provided Tri-C with the freedom to incorporate and evaluate new and existing programs, track progress, adjust course where necessary, and celebrate achievements while continually looking to the future.

In the midst of this deliberate commitment to continuous improvement, the COVID-19 pandemic struck, disrupting the lives of every member of the Cuyahoga community. Like many organizations, the college resorted to operating remotely for a season. But even in this environment, the transformative system we had created accommodated the urgent and unprecedented crisis.

We heightened our commitment to continuous improvement by expanding information technology systems to strengthen online coursework. Services to students, like tutoring and emotional support, became available to them electronically on a 24/7 basis. Computers and tablets were distributed to students who needed the equipment to access their courses. Significant funds were raised to aid students facing crises associated with housing, food, childcare, and other insecurities. Faculty and staff continued to train in coursework design and development for new modes of teaching and service. Classroom spaces were modified to accommodate safe distancing. New fast-track programs were established to prepare displaced workers for new jobs that offered competitive wages. And the college's commitment to providing access to education to individuals in the city's core communities was strengthened through access centers, training and job hubs, and intensive relationships with grassroots organizations.

A year later, as I ready *Capturing Change* for publication, we continue to meet the challenge of COVID-19 and seize the opportunities it provides to advance continuous improvement within the One Door framework. Our five strategic priorities remain intact as the foundation for our work, but the actions to address them are being recalibrated. Reassigning talent, realigning responsibilities, and consolidating resources ensure that the college is prepared to progress in the short and long terms. The student experience is shifting so that work is not an outcome of education but is a starting point—or is integrated throughout in the form of internships and other "earn and learn" opportunities. Innovations in teaching—virtually, in person, or a combination—mean that students can select the modality that coincides with their learning styles. And as we undertake these efforts, targeted recruitment and recovery of diverse and economically disadvantaged students ensure that they can start and continue their education without the disruption of financial and personal hardship. Our community access centers and job hubs will be instrumental in identifying and helping these individuals start on an educational path.

Potential Pitfalls

Among the attributes of continuous improvement through UnCLE is its deliberate nature that allows processes to be improved in real time and change to be introduced gradually. This aspect is often sufficient to reduce barriers—but I would be delusional if I did not acknowledge that potential pitfalls exist.

Inadequate Preparation

Resolving pitfalls rests solely on the shoulders of leaders. This is made easier when they apply the knowledge and tools presented in this book, including the use of vision and strategy to clarify the future and how it will be achieved operationally and through change. These foundations can help reduce distractions and anxiety, leading to trust, commitment to ongoing change, and transformation. The centerpiece for this effort is UnCLE, and it is important that leaders completely understand the model and its benefits. This understanding can serve as the framework for communicating how UnCLE is being applied to improve operations and address change.

Misaligned Vision and Strategy

If there is misalignment between the foundations of vision and strategy and UnCLE, it is possible that change initiatives will be extraneous at best. In all elements of UnCLE, the important AI questions and resulting deliberations should involve everyone so that solutions are developed jointly.

Insufficient Engagement and Collaboration

Engagement and collaboration make it easier to identify valid causes for actions that emanate from internal realities and external sources. This can also help gain support, develop trust, encourage acceptance, and promote teamwork. Without this joint effort, change can be built on faulty premises that contribute to lack of support and, ultimately, to failure.

When identifying strategies and tactics—the second element of UnCLE—it is necessary for the resolutions to actually address the cause for action identified in the first element of UnCLE. Once again, leaders must capitalize on relationships to establish remedies that will be introduced at the ground level, especially when the resolutions involve business process improvements.

Opportunities must be developed for everyone to identify measures. This means that both supporters and critics weigh the outcomes of initiatives, determine success or failure, make modifications or introduce new processes, and celebrate attainments even when they are incremental. This is where the identification of benchmarks and KPIs is important to ensure that everyone understands what success looks like.

Building Transformation on Faulty Outcomes

The first three elements of UnCLE are interrelated, and together they are necessary to address the last element: determining if the organization is prepared for the next wave of refinements and interventions or if there is a need to improve on earlier efforts. This assessment includes evaluating process improvements under the PDCA system to improve operations and sustain change. Once again, this is another important opportunity to gain consensus on what was successful and to then determine what should be the subsequent cause for action.

Leadership Shortcomings

The importance of involving individuals at every level to develop vision and strategy, improve processes, and carry out UnCLE is explicit throughout this section on pitfalls. Over time, this can foster a culture that welcomes deliberate change when moving toward transformation. Leaders occasionally will have to give up control but cannot abdicate responsibility. In the end, they are responsible for all aspects of creating a transformational system, and avoiding pitfalls is among the most efficient ways to carry out this responsibility.

V. Becoming a Leader of Transformation

*"As dealing with change becomes a regular activity,
leading it becomes a skill to hone, an internal capacity to master."*

– Arnaud Henneville

Continuous improvement models, including UnCLE, can be used to promote change within the context of everyday operations. But leaders play a critical role in determining the effectiveness of this process. Clearly, as seen in the number of failed responses to change, not all leaders possess the qualities necessary to lead an organization through transformation. However, I believe these qualities can be taught and developed in any self-regarding leader.

To prepare for this discussion, let's revisit the research reported by John Anderson and his associates in the *Academy of Management Review*. Recall that they validated statistically the effectiveness of Deming's 14 Points as management practice and theory when accounting for seven components:

- Visionary leadership
- Internal and external cooperation
- Learning
- Process management
- Continuous improvement
- Employee fulfillment
- Customer satisfaction

Recall also that two separate follow-up studies validated these components—with an emphasis on visionary leadership. According to the researchers, visionary leaders can leverage these components to establish, practice, and lead a long-term vision for the organization, particularly when:

- The organization engages in non-competitive activities internally and externally
- The organizational capability to recognize and nurture the development of its skills, abilities, and knowledge base is evident
- A set of methodological and behavioral practices emphasizing the management of processes is available

Leading a System of Transformation

With this powerful combination, leaders are equipped to develop a system of transformation. The following summary of a set of characteristics already presented in this book presents what this system looks like:

- The agreed-upon foundational principles, including vision, strategy, and benchmarks (or KPIs) are evident. These necessities promote transformation and can accommodate change in a logical, sequenced, and deliberate fashion supported by process improvements (as seen in UnCLE).

- Human and financial resources are available to carry out actions that are necessary for continuous improvement. People skilled in strategic planning, data management, process development, and evaluation are important to ongoing operations involving change.

- People actively contribute to organizational development, embrace change as a constant, and are proud of even incremental success because they experience how their work has made a difference.

- The organization possesses a culture that believes in and values engagement, transparency, flexibility, and communication. Such a culture can inspire commitment and actually validate progressive and deliberate transformation through continuous improvement.

- Individuals and the organizations are willing to engage in professional development to foster commitment and establish sustainable processes even through leadership transitions.

- An intentional communication plan keeps everyone aware of where the organization is now and where it is headed, with everyone knowledgeable about the roles they play in getting the organization to the destination. As UnCLE elaborates, this understanding is reinforced through foundational principles such as a vision for the future and the ongoing strategies and actions to achieve it.

A transformational system that supports continuous improvement of products and services requires a leader of transformation. This is the right term, as opposed to "transformational leader," for the person responsible for success in this system. A transformational leader's interest is primarily the development of followers, but leaders of transformation are focused on developing the team and strengthening the organization to achieve long-term, sustainable transformation. This responsibility is not just about managing change but about leading institutional development such that change is viewed as a way to advance the organization, not just to solve singular problems. In reinforcing these points, Linda Ackerman Anderson and Dean Anderson conclude that such leaders:

- Correctly position the effort among all of the organization's priorities
- Identify the most catalytic levers for mobilizing action toward the future state
- Set up appropriate participation by all stakeholders in the emergent design of the future state and its implementation
- Clarify comprehensive change infrastructures and leadership roles
- Create effective acceleration strategies and conditions
- Set a realistic pace for the change

Personalizing Leadership

How do leaders of transformation achieve these outcomes? And how can you become such a leader? The first step is understanding the benefits of continuous improvement and the elements of change, as described in the early chapters of this book. Further, any effective leader embodies personal, perhaps more intrinsic, qualities that serve as a foundation for implementing the principles of continuous improvement in a natural, organic manner.

In *Change the Lapel Pin*, I present this type of leadership. This approach can successfully handle change and all of its challenges, especially the important job of leading people. The model gives current and prospective leaders a way to personalize leadership and eliminate faulty, unreliable practices by combining formal training, work experience, and the characteristics of successful leaders—and successful people. The following steps consist of personalizing that knowledge to equip the leader of transformation for this responsibility.

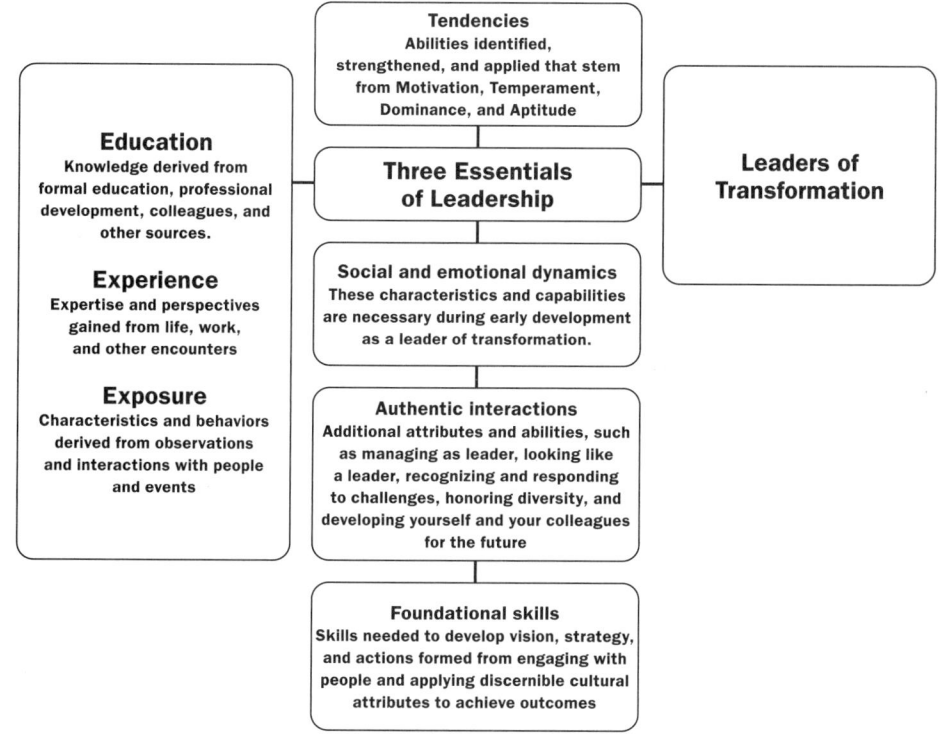

Employing the Three Essentials of Leadership

This combination of influences and factors includes the Three Essentials of Leadership: Education, Experience, and Exposure.

Education is defined as knowledge derived from formal education, professional development, colleagues, and other sources. It allows you, as a leader, to build a core of knowledge that becomes an essential part of your expertise. It is also important that this education not become static. Embracing the notion of "lifelong learning" demonstrates that you view continuous improvement as a model not only for organizational growth but also for personal growth. While this may include pursuing advanced degrees—particularly those that build competency or serve as gatekeepers in your field—formal education is not the only means of following continued educational development. Phil Higson and Anthony Sturgess, authors of the book *Uncommon Leadership: How to Build a Competitive Advantage by Thinking Differently*, illustrate the sources of this knowledge with the following concepts:

- Know your business. There is no substitute for being a student of the business that you are in.

- Know your profession. What are the critical areas of knowledge in your discipline that you need to possess?

- Know your customers. Be in close contact with customers and find out as much as you can about why they deal with your organization.

- Know your colleagues. Build effective relationships—with those who work for you and with a wider network within the organization and at sister institutions.

Experience is defined as the expertise and perspectives gained from life, work, and other encounters. It certainly includes your progression as a leader through various jobs of increasing responsibility, but it should also include taking advantage of opportunities to broaden your experience by volunteering for tasks or work teams outside of your usual duties. All of this expertise is important because it equips you to perform optimally in your current role and prepares you for future opportunities. These experiences often shape your leadership approach, especially when they make you more tactical, deliberate, patient, and sensitive. They allow you to apply your expertise in the crucible of work and beyond.

Exposure represents the characteristics and behaviors derived from observations and interactions with people and events. As you observe others, you will undoubtedly benefit from identifying damaging behaviors you wish to avoid. Determining the superior qualities that you admire and wish to emulate in others can be even more powerful. These may include communication skills, determination to overcome adversity, commitment to collaboration, humility, and more. It is important not only to observe the qualities but also to ascertain how those role models came to develop and strengthen them. Ideally, this will be accomplished through relationships, whether formal mentoring arrangements or informal interactions over the course of time.

As you determine how the Three Essentials of Leadership serve as a basis for your growth as a leader of transformation, it may be helpful to identify key elements that brought you to where you are today and that can dramatically direct the course of your life and work in the future. In recounting these elements, it should be abundantly clear how you have been enriched by them. What has been the impact on your career choice? Has this contributed to your path and ideals about leadership? These are important questions, and the answers will allow you to balance personal characteristics, especially those that foster compassion, with technical skills. Both qualities will be important for your success as a leader of transformation.

Understanding Your Tendencies

To benefit fully from the Three Essentials of Leadership, it is important to identify intuitive capabilities that can help you more fully develop as a leader of transformation. For example, in the article "Origins and Evolution of Leadership," Andrew King, Dominic Johnson, and Mark Van Vugt concluded that individuals emerge as leaders if they exhibit certain tendencies, including motivation, temperament, dominance, and aptitude.

Motivation is one of the traits that can direct group behavior. Motivated leaders are goal-focused and ambitious. They can attract followers who often view them as role models. But sometimes they can be so focused on moving the organization forward that they leave individuals behind.

The *temperament* of leaders often inspires faithful followers because of the personal connection leaders make with others. They are loyal to the organization, promote collaboration, and are trustworthy and ethical. Further, leaders with this attribute are level-headed and well-prepared. Occasionally, however, they are perceived as lacking motivation, having low levels of energy, and boring.

Dominance is a characteristic of leaders who operate more autonomously and are influential within professional and social settings. This trait contributes to self-confidence, risk-taking, and self-reliance. By implication, this characteristic does not naturally embrace collaboration and, therefore, such a leader's actions sometimes appear to be based more on convenient and short-term solutions and less on strategy.

Aptitude in leaders is important when considerable specialized knowledge and training are required. Aptitude reflects purposefulness, conscientiousness, responsibility, and a high level of confidence in one's own abilities. Leaders with this capacity are often frustrated when they cannot arrive at immediate answers to lingering and persistent challenges. They sometimes do not consider what other people think.

As you can see, each characteristic has strengths and shortcomings when considered individually and collectively. According to Heather Fork in an article for *Doctor's Crossing*, it is important to identify and balance traits judiciously in concert with other leadership competencies. This can be accomplished through feedback from thoughtful, candid colleagues and followers and through assessments, including educational psychologist Don Clifton's StrengthsFinder and the 360-Degree Process. Leaders must not only recognize the existence of each attribute and their own tendencies but also when each characteristic naturally emerges and how each can be applied strategically.

Acknowledging Social and Emotional Dynamics

Your emotions will be important as you create and carry out your personalized approach to transformational leadership. This amounts to emotional intelligence—which, according to John Mayer and Peter Salovey in their article for *Intelligence*, is the ability to accurately perceive your own and others' emotions, to understand the signals that emotions send about relationships, and to manage emotions in yourself and others. Coming to grips with your emotional constitution provides a great foundation for important connections with others. You will need this skill to deal with individuals in the organization with a variety of dispositions and to improve "organizational health"—which is defined by Patrick Lencioni, author of *The Advantage: Why Organizational Health Trumps Everything Else in Business*, as high degrees of morale and productivity and very little turnover among employees.

To accomplish this aim, you must first understand your own social and emotional dynamics. Some experts on leadership, such as psychologist and author Daniel Goleman, might refer to this as assessing one's emotional mindset to understand behaviors that might detract from or contribute to success in the workplace.

An online program offered by Mind Tools is among the measures that are available for this assessment. This program applies the principles of emotional intelligence, beginning first with self-awareness, or the ability to identify moods that affect your behavior and impact those around you. In the article "Emotional Intelligence in Leadership," Mind Tools associates suggest that you reflect on your thoughts and slow down to examine why certain people and situations cause an emotional reaction and how you can appropriately react to those encounters. You remain in charge by evaluating what response the situation warrants.

Next in the Mind Tools program is self-regulation, which entails staying in touch with your feelings and the influences that cause stress or anxiety. Leaders who are in control of their feelings can create an environment of trust and fairness. They rely on values, think about the impact on their leadership, and consider where the situation occurred (in a public or private setting). Practicing being calm and allowing an initial emotional reaction in private before addressing the situation can often lead to a more appropriate response.

Following self-regulation is self-motivation, a characteristic that all effective leaders must have. They must be driven to achieve beyond expectations—their own and everyone else's. Leaders of transformation rely heavily on motivation. They often introduce initiatives that build on existing success or create a new sense of urgency to drive personal and organizational renewal.

Next is empathy—the ability to recognize other people's emotions and to understand their perspectives in the process of making intelligent decisions. Empathy translates to putting yourself in someone else's position—an important tool that allows you to relate to individuals on a personal level.

Last in the Mind Tools program is social skills—the ability to build rapport. Social skills are an essential part of leadership that enable you to build good working relationships. Daniel Goleman defines social skills as friendliness with a purpose: moving people in the direction you desire, whether it is agreement on a new marketing strategy or enthusiasm about a new product. Take time to improve your social skills by learning to resolve conflict as it arises across the organization, regardless of its source.

Psychoanalyst and author Manfred F.R. Kets de Vries, in an interview with Diane Coutu in her article "Putting Leaders on the Couch," concludes that emotional intelligence involves a lot more than being introspective. It also involves what Kets de Vries calls the "teddy bear factor": Do people feel comfortable with you? Do they want to be close to you?

Building Skills that Promote Authentic Interactions

The Three Essentials of Leadership, natural tendencies, and emotional intelligence are important foundational qualities for the leader of transformation. These qualities are often underplayed but are always essential to leading organizational operations and change through continuous improvement. They help leaders build consensus through authentic interactions with people, contend with the gradual and deliberate nature of continuous improvement, and deal with the challenges of ongoing process improvement.

However, these attributes do not work alone. They should be applied adroitly to develop and refine other skills that allow you to face the immediate and day-to-day challenges that come with a transformational system. While no such list will be exhaustive, the following sections highlight some examples of those skills.

Communicating and Listening

Communication plays a key role in the process of change, promoting clarity when conveying an organization's vision and helping create and maintain individual connections. Within transformational systems like UnCLE, communication is essential. People need to understand the reasons for change and how they contribute to achieving it through their efforts. It is reassuring—and motivating—when they feel their input is sought and applied. Enlist their involvement up front.

For example, I have used individual meetings with trusted advisors to gain knowledge and have then shared these insights in larger gatherings, notably summits, to elicit feedback, gain consensus, and clarify the work required for success. Ongoing communication keeps everyone updated on progress and allows for further discussions, especially when course corrections are necessary.

To do this effectively, you need to maintain a constant presence and message to motivate and inspire. But it is also important to understand when it is time to listen to the expressions of individuals and groups and perhaps modify your message accordingly. In this context, you must be self-aware and understand how your verbal and nonverbal communications can affect the team.

As such, listening is just as important as speaking. Sara Stibitz, in her article "How to Really Listen to Your Employees," recommends that leaders eliminate distractions that imply that the person speaking and the message are unimportant. You should look for nonverbal cues, like body language, that offer deeper understanding and meaning to the conversation.

While challenging at times, it is important to maintain poise, avoid a rush to judgment, and refrain from immediately offering an opinion while listening. When it is time to react, you should validate and verify the points offered by the speaker and drill down into the conversation to acknowledge what was expressed, regardless of how you feel about it.

Collaborating and Consulting

Collaborative and consultative abilities are essential to building consensus within a system of transformation. In this environment, success depends on everyone working toward an agreed-upon course of action. Along with ongoing communication, collaborating and consulting—when applied proactively—can help counter concerns and contribute to a healthier culture. Simultaneously, this will enable you to recognize and reward individuals who are essential to the success of continuous improvement.

Forbes contributor and consultant Carol Kinsey Gorman emphasizes the importance of collaborating and consulting. She maintains that such engagement is not a "nice-to-have" philosophy. In "8 Tips for Collaborative Leadership," she contends that the approach is essential to productivity in an inclusive environment and that it energizes teams, releases creativity, and makes working together both productive and joyful. It inspires everyone to work toward common goals despite differences in convictions, cultural values, and operating norms.

Advocacy

Being an advocate is another important characteristic that creates an environment in which colleagues feel confident and positive, thus enabling them to perform at their best even under trying conditions. Professional integrity and passion are key attributes of advocacy. In this regard, you are a role model—you set the pace for the rest of the organization, creating a positive and productive working atmosphere. You inspire high—but achievable—expectations and, consequently, infuse high standards of excellence in the organization. Along with a strong work ethic, advocating is one of the most important characteristics of a leader of transformation.

This is an area in which a vision statement can be beneficial as an aspirational, future-oriented goal for the organization. Writing in *Harvard Business Review*, Herminia Ibarra and Morten T. Hansen posit that no company can build a coherent culture without people who either share its core values or possess the willingness and ability to embrace those values. They say that at the heart of leadership advocacy are clearly articulated vision and values that depict where the organization expects to be and the way it pledges to serve clients, treat colleagues, and uphold professional standards. The next section addresses how to create and implement vision.

Commanding Demeanor

A commanding demeanor is often associated with leaders of transformation. These individuals are often described as being motivated, inspired, and polished. These attributes accentuate the message that people have heard over time with clarity and confidence when leaders are representing and articulating the organization's vision, core values, and operational principles. For new leaders, a professional development course that incorporates public speaking lessons can offer a head start on developing the mannerisms necessary in the leadership role.

Consistent Messaging

An ally to a commanding demeanor is consistent messaging. When done properly, it is perhaps one of the most powerful tools a leader can possess. Why? Because it allows for presenting in a few words what the organization strives to accomplish, how it can be done, and by whom.

Consistent messaging is also a way for leaders to assert their hopes and aspirations for the organization. It allows others to embrace a common vision, know the direction of the organization, and understand how all work is valued and contributes to successful outcomes. In this context, the culture of the organization transforms to incorporate the language emphasized in the leader's message. Author E.D. Hirsch popularized this phenomenon as "cultural literacy": the ability to understand and participate fluently in a given (organizational) culture.

Acting and Doing

Consistent messaging should be modeled—the expression that comes to mind is "walking the talk," or demonstrating beliefs through actions and deeds. Sometimes this is represented by reallocating resources to fund initiatives. Another way to build support for the message is to connect with individuals throughout the organization to seek and use their advice and recommendations.

Providing periodic updates through public appearances, such as town hall meetings, publications, and social media, shows commitment to an agreed-upon course of action. Your physical presence both inside and outside the organization can more firmly establish your identity. Being active in professional organizations provides an opportunity to learn from and contribute to the global dialogue about running an organization. Involvement in other networks created through social and business interactions, such as nonprofit boards, provides further enrichment and exposure.

Observation

Besides acting and doing, being observant is one of the most important attributes a leader can possess. Noticing details and recognizing patterns can help them to be proactive when addressing challenges and responding to trends.

The result of being an observant leader is understanding what Carol Cartwright, president emerita of Kent State University, calls the "rhythm of the organization." This heightened awareness takes time to develop, but once established, it allows leaders to intuit what they expect to be there, recognize what is there, and notice what is not there. It is discerning the heart of the organization, its tempo, and its energy and perceiving where it may be out of sync.

So how do you develop these capabilities? First, understanding people is essential to becoming a more observant leader. Determining what motivates them, discovering their preferred communication methods, and identifying why they are succeeding (or not) helps a leader establish a baseline. Variations from this baseline—positive or negative—can then be identified more readily.

Once you understand people, it is imperative to create stronger personal connections that allow you to feel comfortable in open and honest dialogue. This may later help uncover misunderstanding and defuse conflict. In the process, individuals believe their point of view has been heard. Other important outcomes are building trust and respect in an atmosphere of problem-solving and improved teamwork.

Finally, demonstrate being observant through active listening—concentrating on what is being said by using verbal and nonverbal messages, such as maintaining eye contact, nodding your head, smiling, and encouraging the speaker to continue. When receiving this feedback, the person speaking will usually feel more at ease and will perhaps communicate more easily, openly, and honestly.

Establishing Direction through Vision, Strategy, and Outcomes

Organizational foundations—including vision, strategies, and benchmarks—must be evident to incorporate change as a part of everyday operations. These foundations are essential as leaders seek to create systems of transformation aided by UnCLE and the leadership qualities discussed in this chapter.

A bold vision is important for the ascent of an organization and is a synopsis for a future. It undergirds the mission, providing a more tangible framework for carrying out and weighing the effectiveness of the organization.

The vision is also important because it allows you to convey your aspirations for the organization in a few words. It should be based on a deep understanding and appreciation of global issues and perspectives, enunciated by you, which gives it credence as the guidepost for progress through continuous improvement.

Kamran Akbarzadeh, author of *Leadership Soup: A Healthy Yet Tasty Recipe for Living and Leading on Purpose*, contends that a vision statement should add value by inspiring action. According to Akbarzadeh, when people read a positive statement, it fills them with positive energy that connects them to the organization. To inspire this response, the vision statement should be:

- **In the present tense**—Vision refers to visualizing the future and painting it in the present.

- **Short**—Lengthy vision descriptions typically lose their impact and may cause people to disconnect. Short and clear, yet rich and powerful, vision statements are easy to remember and communicate.

- **Challenging**—Powerful vision testimonies motivate people to achieve something bigger.

- **Attractive**—If people cannot relate to the vision, it is like having no vision at all.

I will add to this collection of descriptors that it should be measurable. Each element must be assessed to determine the extent to which it contributes to creating and sustaining a transformational system.

To put the vision into effect, a strategic plan or approach is necessary. It helps leaders identify and respond to the opportunities or challenges that, if overlooked, can stifle productivity and limit transformation. Strategy is necessary to keep the organization on course by creating and implementing a response, determining the effectiveness of the intervention, and determining how the results can guard against inaction.

UnCLE is the perfect tool for this exercise that is key to continuous improvement. It fosters vision and strategy that promote outcomes based on internal and external norms, standards, and benchmarks that are the basis for the next wave of organizational refinements and innovations.

Building and Sustaining Your Foundation

In this section of *Capturing Change*, my intent was to provide an understanding of the foundational principles needed to start your journey toward becoming a leader of transformation. While it is important to understand the power and value of continuous improvement, I believe the personalized leadership approach presented in *Change the Lapel Pin* is a way to acknowledge and develop the authenticity required to work effectively with people, practices, and processes as part of continuous improvement.

These are important foundations for a leader, for they allow your team to view you as a constant. Your consistent messages and actions permit others to know and understand your leadership approach and the direction for the organization. These actions also assist in developing a heightened awareness of the organization and the small but important matters that serve either to derail or support continuous improvement. Your physical presence throughout the organization and beyond helps affirm your personal commitment to institutional and community advancement.

This last point bears repeating: You *must* undertake a concerted effort to ensure your closer proximity to individuals who carry out day-to-day operations and who often know firsthand how to address specific challenges and opportunities. This is where you can gain additional respect and support by flattening the organization, either structurally or perceptually, allowing you to develop stronger ties with coalitions of respected individuals who can advise you on important matters and represent the interests and opinions of their colleagues. Be sure to listen and respond. Emphasize that the group promotes collective engagement and not individual interests that should be addressed through existing channels.

Further, pay attention to the culture of the system. Be aware of the powerful values and beliefs that can affect behavior and productivity and bring various factions together. This is where a cultural assessment can be helpful. First, it can be used to promote involvement that leads to a culture of teamwork and understanding. It can improve consistency because clear expectations are set by the leader and adhered to at every phase of the change process. It can enhance adaptability, leading to a culture of openness and flexibility to accommodate both anticipated and unexpected change. The assessment can also promote communication, enabling employees to be aware of the organization's progress toward transformation.

Being visible and approachable is an opportunity to be known on a personal level and to display interpersonal skills that complement technical expertise. Encourage managers to apply similar approaches in their divisions and departments, which fosters greater levels of commitment and productivity across the organization.

In the book *Radical Change, the Quiet Way*, Debra Meyerson describes transformation in two ways: through drastic action, as in change management, and through evolutionary adaptation, as in continuous improvement. In the former, change is discontinuous and often forced on the organization by top management, happens quickly, and often involves significant pain. Evolutionary change, by contrast, is gentle, incremental, and decentralized, and over time it produces a broad and lasting shift with less upheaval. Meyerson describes leaders of evolutionary change as "tempered radicals" who "gently push against prevailing norms, making a difference in small but steady ways and setting examples from which others can learn." She goes on to say, "The changes they inspire are so incremental that they barely merit notice. Like drops of water, these approaches are innocuous enough in themselves. But, over time and in accumulation, they can erode granite."

Meyerson's description of tempered radicals is exactly how leaders of transformation should be viewed. Their interests are totally focused on change for organizational advancement. They apply a multitude of approaches, like UnCLE, to formalize change. Their influence is important in enlisting others to both support and implement actions. They are not looking for accolades but are willing to trumpet the achievements of others. They are committed to transformation but recognize that flexibility is necessary within certain parameters. They are able to draw in both champions and detractors. And as they confront pitfalls, they revert back to vision, strategy, and outcomes to rechart the course to transformation.

Authenticity in a Leader of Transformation—Howard Schultz

Consider an example of a leader of transformation whose personal attributes and professional characteristics inspired individuals to be part of a collective team working toward transformation: Howard Schultz, who headed Starbucks, one of the most successful businesses in the world. His profile was briefly included in *Change the Lapel Pin* as an example of how to champion diversity as a CEO in a large multinational company.

Subsequent to that book's publication, I had the privilege of interviewing Schultz in February 2019 during his visit to Parma, Ohio. He was there to promote his latest book, *From the Ground Up: A Journey to Reimagine the Promise of America*, and perhaps to gain perspective for a potential presidential campaign. Schultz and I enjoyed a brief conversation during which he asked how America could upgrade salaries for teachers, improve student success in mathematics and science, and increase degree attainment. As an educator, I was embarrassed that my answers were not textbook quality. But I was humbled that a leader of Schultz's stature would ask those questions and choose me to interview him.

That interaction confirmed what I had read about Schultz—that he seeks answers everywhere. When I extend this quality to his leadership, I imagine it builds confidence, motivates followers to solve problems, and allows him to address issues head on. This is how leaders of transformation act, says Joseph Chris in his blog "Seven Howard Schultz Leadership Style Principles." According to Chris, Schultz's vision—much like Amazon CEO Jeff Bezos'—is to build a company that is focused on treating employees and customers with respect and dignity. These stakeholders are the pillars of Starbucks, beginning with the baristas who give a personal touch to customers. Baristas offer ideas that improve services and products—and their own creations are periodically featured in national campaigns such as #baristaoriginals.

Underlying Schultz's vision for Starbucks are processes that help carry it out. First, he believes in hiring the right people. He promotes hiring employees who have intuitive leadership skills that enhance the customer experience.

Second, with more than 22,000 stores globally, Starbucks' various coffee blends remain consistent. This consistency extends to the stores and branding, including food and amenities such as Wi-Fi.

Third, a commitment to diversity in employees, suppliers, and owners has an important place in Schultz's leadership approach. He believes that Starbucks should reflect the growing diversity of a multicultural world and contribute to the economic development of the communities it serves.

Fourth, Schultz believes that finding the right partner makes it easier to expand the company's market. For example, Starbucks joined forces with Barnes & Noble to set up combined businesses at many locations, including campus bookstores.

Although Schultz is a leader of transformation, he did not initially leave behind a system of transformation. Following his first retirement in 2000, some of his ideas that were evident in the Starbucks brand were discontinued. For example, Starbucks ceased grinding its own coffee. In opting for flavor-locked bags, the company lost one of its greatest and most powerful nonverbal signals: its legendary "aroma." With a brand harmed by this and other changes, the company's stock tanked.

In early 2008, Schultz returned for his second stint as CEO. He closed underperforming stores, retrained employees, and discontinued breakfast foods that competed with the coffee aroma. His strategies worked, and the stock recovered—gaining 143 percent in 2009.

In 2017, Schultz passed the reins of Starbucks, now a system of transformation, to his hand-picked successor, Kevin Johnson.

Like other leaders of transformation who have personalized their leadership, Schultz's experiences, education, and exposures served as the platform for his success. Schultz grew up in public housing in the blue-collar Canarsie section of Brooklyn. When he was seven years old, his father suffered a broken foot on the job but had no health insurance or worker's compensation. According to Shana Lenowitz in *Business Insider*, Schultz believed that his tremendous professional success was in a way a tribute to his father, who never attained fulfillment and dignity from work that he found meaningful. Schultz realized his experience needed to be different than his parents'.

After graduating from Northern Michigan University and holding several jobs, Schultz encountered Starbucks when he was working for a manufacturer of drip coffee makers. He eventually met Starbucks owners Gerald Baldwin and Gordon Bowker and was so taken with their passion and courage that he went to work for them. He eventually purchased the company in 1987 for $3.8 million. Today, thanks to Schultz's development of the company into a system of transformation, Starbucks is valued at an estimated $84.6 billion, and Schultz's personal net worth is at least $3 billion.

VI. Requirements for and Drivers of Change

*"Change is the law of life. And those who look
only to the past or present are certain to miss the future."*

– John F. Kennedy

In addition to having immense demands placed on them, leaders of transformation must also possess more than a cursory knowledge of the instigators of change and then determine the impact of those factors on fulfilling the greatest incentive for change—increasing customer numbers and satisfaction.

Attention to customers requires organizations to adapt and innovate regularly. Michael Treacy and Fred Wiersema, authors of *The Discipline of Market Leaders*, summarize the challenge of satisfying contemporary consumers as "when good is not enough." Customers increasingly seek high quality at low cost, and Treacy and Wiersema contend that when it comes to customer service as a competitive advantage:

- As costs rise, it is no longer possible to pass those increases on to customers; in fact, costs must be maintained or even lowered as quality increases in order to accommodate rising customer expectations.

- Customers look for more than hassle-free service; they must have effortless, flawless, and instantaneous performance.

- It is not possible to assume that good basic service is sufficient; customers demand premium service, regardless of what they pay.

- Compromising on quality and product capabilities is no longer acceptable; products must be built to deliver nothing less than superiority and unsurpassed innovation.

In this environment, gaining customer (and often investor) loyalty is the preeminent goal of transformation, regardless of the size and nature of the enterprise. Leaders must be attuned to factors that contribute to this end. I call the factors inside the organization "requirements for change" and those external to the organization "drivers of change." As you consider the sources, and in accordance with the familiar SWOT (Strengths, Weaknesses, Opportunities, and Threats) analysis, it is helpful to think of strengths and weaknesses as requirements for change from inside the organization, while opportunities and threats represent drivers of change outside the organization.

Requirements for Change

When thinking about requirements for change, consider those factors that lead to a system of transformation prepared for any eventuality. For this to happen, it is necessary to have in place foundations of vision and strategy, business processes that are evaluated on a consistent basis, a rigorous continuous improvement framework like UnCLE, and people committed to promoting change through their participation and effort. Most importantly, an organization requires a leader who can identify and communicate the external opportunities and threats or the trends that affect transformation.

Even in this dynamic environment where change is no stranger, the leader of transformation must pay attention to how even small modifications can affect progress. For example, in changing a business process in one area, the action could impact a process used in another location, possibly leading to misalignment and frustration. As business processes are improved, administrative procedures, rules, and regulations need to be overhauled as well. Structural changes that increase efficiency, profitability, and cost savings fall into this category.

In a time of rapid change, being cognizant of how people respond is important. While the vast majority may be comfortable with the pace of transformation, others may not. Questions concerning the impact on individuals' career growth and job security must be addressed truthfully to allay fear and anxiety and to help people make personal decisions about the future.

I will later discuss technology as a driver of change. But as a requirement of change *inside* the organization, technology can be used to upgrade work processes, apply automation to mundane tasks, or improve customer service. As processes are revamped, retraining employees for different jobs or implementing new recruiting and hiring practices may be necessary.

All these actions make it possible to prepare for the more volatile drivers of change discussed in the next section. More specifically, as Faye Chua explains in "Drivers of Change in the U.S.," they allow for a wide range of possibilities, like building tolerance for uncertainty, sparking curiosity about what's around the corner, and developing a truly global operating model.

Drivers of Change

Playing a very prominent role in determining internal requirements for change are external drivers of change. When properly understood and accounted for, these drivers help achieve long-lasting benefits. Therefore, it is important that leaders of transformation fully understand their impact and how to respond to them.

A natural disaster such as COVID-19 is one example of these drivers. Even in the face of the pandemic, which led to shuttered businesses, historically high unemployment rates, and volatile financial markets, the possibility of significant strides in health care and medicine emerged. This demonstrates that such an emergency can still lead to opportunity and transformation.

Although I have alluded to some drivers in earlier chapters, it is worthwhile to invest time exploring certain drivers more fully and discussing how they may present both challenges and opportunities for leaders of transformation. These selected drivers reach across industry sectors and reflect ongoing change that shows no indication of slackening.

Technology

The driver most often cited by organizational experts is technology, which will have an unending impact on society now and in the future. Patrick Gleeson, in "Factors That May Cause Change in an Organization," suggests that the technology an organization uses on an everyday basis can be outdated in as little as a few months. Consequently, leaders need to be responsive to advances and their influence on society and the workplace. As an illustration, the World Economic Forum concludes in its report "Drivers of Change" that the growth in widespread and affordable computing power, especially the ubiquity of access to the Internet through mobile and voice-activated devices, has already had widespread impact on how customers are choosing to acquire products and services.

Technological trends, the far-ranging implications of which have not yet fully materialized, are expected to be well under way in specific industries in the coming years. In "Eight Ways Technology Is Changing Business," Orrin Broberg provides examples of how technology might look and be applied in the near future:

- Mobility is a big thing, and Google, for example, is responding by making mobile web browsing easier, facilitating business remotely, and satisfying everyday needs through the use of a smart device or tablet.

- Cloud computing will continue to allow many types of organizations to move some of their operations to third-party servers accessible through Internet connectivity. This has allowed small businesses to access resources that would be too costly if purchased individually. It has also leveled the competition against organizations with more funding for technology.

- Cloud computing will not only economize the storage of data but will also increase the flow and analysis of data. Such analysis permits organizations to segment customers, identify specific needs, and target marketing to previously impossible degrees. Broberg says that even a simple Google account allows for determining where visitors to websites come from, what type of browser they are using, how they found the website, what they do while on it, how long they stay, and at which point they decide to leave.

- Technology has increased the ability to interact through text and video at a moment's notice, which has implications for communicating with customers in real time and improving job productivity, an aspect that has been expedited as a result of the COVID-19 pandemic.

- Hardware and software will be acquired at more affordable rates and become simple enough to use that businesses need not hire dedicated employees or sign long-term service contracts. Tech-savvy entrepreneurs may see this as an opportunity to build and expand businesses.

- Among those taking on these new business opportunities are millennials, who are becoming the primary driving force behind business, the economy, and the world. They were raised on digital technology, are the most wired adult generation, and are primarily responsible for forcing business to become more tech-supported.

- Social networking has given businesses a more affordable and accessible means of communicating in real time, which has the potential to expand exponentially with the emergence of 5G networks.

- Consumers have unfettered access to social media and use it liberally to offer opinions on just about everything, including customer relationships. In this environment, "OK" customer service and product offerings will not suffice and can actually contribute to poor and angry reviews. Amazon is among the online companies that have made customer service a major focus. Through its Amazon Prime program, in particular, millions of individuals get customized treatment, access to a range of products at discounted prices, and free or reduced shipping costs.

These examples are presented with the knowledge that they will quickly become outdated—which, of course, only serves to prove the point. The prescience of many of these observations was proven as the COVID-19 pandemic quickly pushed both organizations and individuals to embrace technology to an unparalleled degree. For example, at my college, we were forced to adapt to the closing of our classrooms and facilities, and employees began working from home. Faculty transitioned to remote instruction, requiring extensive use of videoconferencing in the form of Webex, Zoom, Google Teams, online instruction tools, and digital communication. This move exposed the extent of the digital divide—access to technology and especially broadband Internet access was a problem for workers and students residing in certain urban and rural communities. Unless this situation is rectified, economic inequality, which is already a serious problem, will escalate dramatically.

The omnipresence of technology means there is no way that organizations can avoid its impact on operations and growth. Its rapid advancement can challenge leaders as they decide what technology will benefit the organization now and in the near future. In an environment where change is constant, though, it may be preferable to choose technology to augment, as opposed to lead, strategic direction and growth. This can keep organizations from becoming too dependent on technology. In this vein, Gleeson concludes, "You have to understand how technology affects your business (for better or worse) and how to apply advancements in order to play them to your advantage."

Demographic and Socioeconomic Trends

The World Economic Forum report indicates that demographic and socioeconomic shifts are expected to have nearly as strong an impact on business models and organizational structures as technology. Emerging markets, increased geopolitical volatility, and the need to transition toward an environmentally sustainable economy are all seen as major drivers of change in this area.

Emerging Economies

For years, large sums of money have been invested in emerging economies on the premise that places like China, India, other markets in Asia, and Latin America could develop their resources more quickly with foreign capital. This was seen as potentially providing a high rate of return and diversification to investors, especially in countries where the political climates have been favorable.

However, financial returns from these investments diminished, starting with a severe drop during the 2008–2009 crisis that precipitated a global slowdown and reduced investments in emerging economies. Nonetheless, Rohit Chopra and Juan Mier of Lazard Asset Management believe this did not deter investors from seeing renewed opportunities in these nations going forward. Broadly speaking, economic growth in emerging markets outpaced developed markets in 2017, and certain factors may continue widening their growth margin. Gonzalo Pangaro, Michael Cornelius, and Ernest Yeunge of T. Rowe Price believe the following trends will be evident:

- Emerging countries in Southeast Asia are leading the way in enacting reforms and correcting the fundamental imbalances that made them vulnerable in past financial crises. India and Indonesia, in particular, have made notable progress in implementing needed reforms, making capital flows strong into the future. While volatility is likely to remain in the short to medium term for some Latin American countries, long-term equity investment opportunities in the region are anticipated because of a broad shift toward political leaders who tend to implement investor-friendly policies.

- Countries in emerging Europe are broadly behind other regions in terms of their willingness and ability to make meaningful reforms. The governments of Russia and Turkey are key offenders.

A word of caution here is that another financial downturn could be problematic—and as this book is being written, the long-term economic effects of the pandemic remain uncertain. So, as proposed by Martin Reeves and Johann Harnoss in "An Agenda for the Future of Global Business," it will be important to focus on investing in emerging markets whose growth is not too dependent on commodity prices but comes instead from consumer-oriented industries such as health care.

Another factor that may impede growth in emerging economies is the rise of economic nationalism. This was exemplified in former President Donald Trump's "America First" policies that called for tariffs, championed the walling off of Mexico, and threatened withdrawal from the longstanding North American Free Trade Agreement. The controversial plan by the United Kingdom to withdraw from the European Union (EU), or "Brexit," is another example of such populism beyond U.S. borders, based as it was on the pretext that membership in the EU was undermining socially conservative political beliefs, supporting open immigration, and making life in Britain worse.

This rise of populism must be factored in as leaders contemplate doing business in emerging markets. This will require them to commit to supporting economic and social progress to strengthen their enterprises for the long term. For many companies, according to Witold Heinzs and Bennet Zelner in "Emerging Markets," this entails looking beyond just the quick cost-benefit analysis of such transactions and considering both the financial and social benefits, based on the premise that globalization is a major driver of growth and prosperity for everyone.

Environmentally Sustainable Economy

The ecosystem is increasingly seen as providing the natural resources that fuel financial growth, making economic activity and the environment interdependent. This viewpoint, which is essentially different from recent policy that treats economy and ecology independently, is a key feature of environmentally sustainable economic development. The goal of this movement is to satisfy the needs of capital and wealth accumulation in a manner that sustains natural resources and the environment for future generations.

The interplay between the economy and the environment should be a factor in organizational change, leading to a focus on investments that produce both financial and social benefit. An example of this duality comes from Barry Dalal-Clayton and Stephen Bass, authors of the report

"Sustainable Development through Regional Economic Strategies," who believe that an environmentally sustainable economy will reflect processes for manufacturing goods and providing services that are environmentally benign across their life cycle. These practices reduce material and energy consumption, resulting in cost savings that can be reinvested to make companies more financially secure, more competitive, and equipped to produce more jobs. Sustainable practices also improve workplaces and communities, making them healthier, less toxic, and more pleasant places to be.

Geopolitical Volatility

In an interview in *Leaders* magazine, Jim Thomas of Zurich Insurance Group says that latent political risks are not unusual and that the high-visibility risks raise greater concern. The issues with emerging economies and populist movements, as reflected in the examples of America First and Brexit, are certainly among these occurrences. The refugee crisis in Syria, ongoing conflict in the Middle East, and China's economic sluggishness have all shaped the geopolitical landscape in recent years as well. Even though China's economy has continued to experience stronger growth than the rest of the world, international stock markets came to a virtual standstill when China's market temporarily dropped, significantly resetting global trade dynamics.

Some may believe that the United States is immune to such vulnerabilities. It is not, mostly due to the interconnectedness of the global economy. Also, the country could experience internal volatility if certain conditions were evident. David Anderson of Zurich Insurance Group believes that interstate conflict, such as state collapse or crisis, failure of national governance, terror attacks, and natural disasters present conditions in which the country could struggle to maintain critical infrastructure such as power grids, transportation nodes, and emergency services.

We have experienced these incidents in small doses, particularly when Hurricanes Harvey, Irma, and Maria occurred within 60 days of one another in 2017. Mark Avallone, writing for *Forbes*, found that the storms led to unemployment, decreased economic viability, and annihilated infrastructures in Texas, Florida, and especially Puerto Rico. On a national scale, the gross domestic product (GDP) was affected as a result of the hurricanes, and the recovery cost reached $200 billion. Moreover, a federal government shutdown due to the past failure of the U.S. Congress to pass a budget is evidence of what can happen when there is not bipartisan leadership in Washington. Critical services and programs are shut down and workers are furloughed, thus heightening anxiety and uncertainty among taxpayers.

The community shutdowns due to the 2020 pandemic introduced major shocks to stability worldwide. This was especially true in the United States, which has seen uneven public health and economic measures on both the state-to-state and national levels as well as protests over the closures. In the midst of the pandemic, the murder of George Floyd touched off renewed and powerful calls against racism, with a particular focus on the relationship between police and communities that led to nationwide protests both peaceful and violent. And then the rhetoric and actions surrounding the 2020 presidential election became increasingly incendiary, leading to the January 6, 2021, siege on the U.S. Capitol. The implications and ultimate outcomes of these and other recent circumstances are yet to be discerned.

Geopolitical risks are particularly challenging. They are hard to predict, and their results can cascade into many other risks. But as indicated in "Disruptive Trends: Geopolitics" by KPMG, economic and political risks should be accounted for if organizational change is to be fully established. To do so, organizations must still anticipate and understand the risk, address how it will be mitigated, determine if existing internal risk management controls are effective, and identify whether more controls are necessary.

Government Regulations

Even when geopolitical circumstances are more stable, government economic policy and regulations have an influence on the competitiveness and profitability of businesses. And as businesses become more complex, the nature of government's relationship to them may become increasingly interconnected as well. In this vein, Marc Davis writes in *Investopedia* that when a change in government takes place—for example, when a new president is elected and a new administration is installed—a new political agenda may be introduced. This was certainly the case with President Donald Trump's "Make America Great Again" philosophy, which purportedly was to restore the country to its "former glory."

Examples of the actions to carry out his ideology included attempts to dismantle the Affordable Care Act enacted during President Barack Obama's administration and efforts to overhaul immigration policies such as the Deferred Action for Childhood Arrivals, which was also enacted by President Obama and ruled appropriate by the U.S. Supreme Court.

It will be particularly interesting to see how President Trump's 2018 tax reform measure, labeled the Tax Cut and Jobs Act, will accomplish organizational change in the long term. According to Joe Ciolli in *Business Insider*, most economists identified a boost to the U.S. economy in the short term. But the size and length of that boost, with estimates ranging from 0.008 to 0.12 percent over the next decade according to financial experts and government officials, may not be the 3 percent growth and large increases in wages promised by supporters of the tax bill.

With respect to individual taxpayers, most American households received a tax cut that more substantially benefited wealthier citizens. Ciolli puts this tax cut in perspective by providing an example from Howard Gleckman, a senior fellow at the Tax Policy Center, who remarked, "For middle-income people, the extra $900 they saved in taxes paid for about seven months of gas. By contrast, those in the top 1 percent could pick up a nice Mercedes C-Class Coupe with their $50,000 average tax cut."

Ciolli asserts that the biggest benefit of the tax bill for businesses was a cut in the federal corporate tax rate from 35 percent to 21 percent. As a consequence, Amazon, Google, and Facebook alone possibly saved $4.5 billion in taxes in 2018, and the stock market saw a serious increase of $10 per share of S&P companies during the same year.

A significant unanswered question is how businesses will use the increase in profits. Some government officials claimed that the increased profits would eventually be spent on capital investments like new factories and higher wages. For example, after the bill's final passage, some major companies like Comcast, Boeing, and AT&T announced bonuses and wage increases stemming from the tax bill. This may be somewhat consistent with how companies in general say they would apply the savings now and in the future. But based on reporting by Randy Kiersz in *Business Insider*, the results of a survey by the Federal Reserve of Atlanta indicate that:

- 59 percent of business executives said the legislation would lead to "no change" in their employment plans.

- 31 percent said they would increase hiring "somewhat," and 8 percent said they would increase hiring "significantly."

- 11 percent said they would significantly increase capital investment, 40 percent said they would increase investment somewhat, and 46 percent said there would be no change in their plans.

Kiersz concluded that overall, the survey did seem to indicate a bias toward increased spending on the part of businesses. However, it remains unclear what effect the COVID-19 pandemic will have on these plans, including how these Trump-era policies will interact with the stimulus checks and other additional government spending during the pandemic and potentially beyond, including the more comprehensive, costlier stimulus package that was passed by Congress early in President Joseph Biden's term.

Competition

In 1992, WalMart passed Sears to become the world's number one retailer. How did Sears allow this to happen? Langdon Morris, in "The Driving Forces of Change," concludes that Sears suffered from the arrogant assumption that it was invulnerable, and then its leaders fundamentally misunderstood the key competitive dynamics in the market and allowed WalMart to out-innovate them in three critical performance dimensions: cost of goods, cost of distribution, and pricing.

The Sears example touches on only one of the forces used to eliminate competition—commoditization, or the inexorable pressure that drives prices downward. In his seminal 1979 article "How Competitive Forces Shape Strategy," Michael Porter asserts that there are competitive forces that go well beyond the established combatants in a particular industry. Customers, suppliers, potential entrants, and substitute products are all competitors that may be more or less prominent or active depending on the industry. Here is how Porter views the impact that these four categories have on competition:

- Rivalry among existing competitors takes the familiar form of jockeying for customers—using tactics like price competition, product introduction, and advertising slugfests. Suppliers can exert bargaining power on participants in an industry by raising prices or reducing the quality of purchased goods and services. Powerful suppliers can thereby squeeze profitability out of an industry that is unable to recover cost increases in retail prices.

- New entrants to an industry bring new capacity, the desire to gain market share, and often substantial resources.

- Substitute products or services limit the potential of an industry. Unless substitutes can upgrade the quality of the product or differentiate it somehow, the industry will suffer in earnings and possibly in growth.

Porter asserts that knowledge of these underlying sources of competitive pressure provides the groundwork for a strategic agenda of action that highlights the critical strengths and weaknesses of an organization. It helps create strategies for the organization's positioning in its industry, clarifies the areas where strategic changes may yield the greatest payoff, and highlights the places where industry trends promise to hold the greatest significance as either opportunities or threats.

Understanding and applying these elements allow organizations to stake out a position that is less vulnerable to attack from head-to-head opponents, whether established or new, and less vulnerable to erosion from the direction of buyers, suppliers, and substitute goods. Establishing such a position can take many forms—solidifying relationships with favorable customers, differentiating the product either substantively or psychologically through marketing, integrating forward or backward, or establishing technological leadership.

Diversity

For decades, businesses have touted the virtues of a diverse workplace, often with only cursory results. Many efforts have faltered because they have been poorly led, implemented, and resourced.

These failures perpetuate existing biases on the job. For example, perceptual, cultural, and language barriers continue to persist due to the inability of leaders to communicate the key objectives, teamwork, and commitment required to make diversity a value proposition. Further, some individuals still refuse to accept that the social and cultural makeup of society and the workplace is changing. This attitude—that "we've always done it this way"—is counterproductive since it silences new ideas and inhibits progress. In addition, workplace policies are often ineffective because they are built on inaccurate metrics that prevent appropriately customized strategies and programs. Finally, diversity training alone is not sufficient to create an effective program across every department and function of the organization.

This has to change if organizations wish to be competitive now and in the future. Why? First, organizations have an opportunity to demonstrate in the workplace that acknowledging and celebrating differences among people is healthy and rewarding. Diversity, as an outcome of America's civil rights movement, is still an important tool for achieving equality and mitigating the vestiges of discrimination. Second, diversity is essential to increasing profits while simultaneously promoting social and economic good. With a surge in customers across many demographic lines, embracing diversity is a condition for success in a global economy.

Some companies, like those identified by DiversityInc in its annual list of top corporations for diversity, understand and promulgate the value proposition of this driver of change. DiversityInc identifies in these businesses the best practices that other organizations can adapt and expand upon, such as:

- **CEO involvement**—While many companies have a chief diversity officer or a head of human services who oversees diversity, the companies that stand out are those in which the CEO is actively engaged.

- **Technology as a diversity tool**—Companies are using technology platforms to facilitate diversity programs.

- **Affinity groups**—Companies create affinity groups for workers who fit into a variety of categories, including race, gender, disability, age, and sexual orientation.

- **Supplier diversity**—Suppliers are required to reflect diversity in their values to ensure that the supply chain honors the organization's commitment to diversity.

The murder of George Floyd by a Minneapolis police officer, which was witnessed by millions of Americans on national television, sparked protests by citizens across racial and ethnic lines. This unfortunate event, however, may actually heighten commitment to diversity. Some CEOs were compelled (often by their employees) to issue statements condemning the killing and vowing to make a strategic imperative of improving racial equity and promoting healing in the workplace and beyond. Among them is Doug Baker of Ecolab, who says in a statement issued on June 9, 2020:

> *George Floyd has been laid to rest. I hope this begins the process of comfort and closure for his family. I know this won't bring closure to the underlying issues laid bare by Mr. Floyd's death: racism, unequal opportunities, and outright physical abuse targeted to our black community.*

What remains to be seen is how Baker and other CEOs intend to back these words with actions that recognize the diversity of their consumers, highlight the qualities of those consumers as workers, and create connections within the communities where these consumers live.

An example of what I hope will occur comes from cigarette and tobacco manufacturer Philip Morris International (PMI). PMI has incorporated diversity into its strategic focus, with the intent to transform into a science and technology leader in smoke-free products for the millions of diverse people who would otherwise continue smoking. To be successful, the company seeks to unlock the creativity and innovation within its workforce, using inclusion and diversity to accomplish its mission in the following ways:

- **Developing a creative and innovative organization**—Through a diverse and inclusive environment that helps drive creativity and innovation, PMI will unleash its collective talent to help solve society's most pressing complex problems.

- **Achieving change through diverse leadership**—These leaders embody empathy, among other human qualities, overcome challenges, and develop leadership styles that integrate work and personal priorities.

- **Driving change in science through diversity**—Research and innovation are at the center of PMI's business transformation as it advances toward a smoke-free future. Diversity is important for reaching all adult smokers who do not quit as PMI delivers a benefit to society and public health.

Diversity has many immediate and tangible benefits, but more work is required to attain this goal in both the workplace and society.

In summarizing requirements and drivers of change, I turn to Firas Kittaneh, a contributor to *Entrepreneur*. Kittaneh believes that leaders who thrive under pressure from inside and outside the organization pave the way to a stronger competitive position. Instead of viewing disruption as an obstacle, these leaders see it as a way to improve goodwill, loyalty, and trust by consumers, as well as a method to position the organization as an indispensable influencer for catalyzing true social progress. A continuous improvement environment is the way to achieve this status.

VII. Models of Change: Case Studies on Transformational Systems

*"The most important thing to remember is this:
… be ready at any moment to give up what you are for
what you might become."*

– W.E.B. Du Bois

Improving internal processes to integrate external drivers of change can result in increased consumer loyalty and satisfaction, improved products and profits, and strong brand recognition. To achieve this end at the highest level takes time and effort. Continuous improvement is certainly an aid to this end—and is perhaps essential, thanks to its support of both measured and immediate responses to change. This result comes when leaders can implement and oversee systems of transformation in which change is natural, healthy, and welcomed.

There are examples of such systems in practice, including the "Transformation 20" companies recognized in 2020 by Innosight, a strategy and innovation business that empowers forward-thinking organizations to navigate disruptive change and own the future. The 20 companies are noted for how they responded to disruptive change by adapting to create additional growth around new products, services, or business models in areas such as digital transformation, climate change, financial technology (fintech), and health care. Innosight has termed the 20 companies "transformational organizations."

By probing deeply into the companies, Innosight recognizes five characteristics that distinguish them and their leaders. First, they created a higher-purpose mission by infusing through words and deeds the need and benefit of transformation. Second, they were willing to build upon successes of the past but were not afraid to redeploy resources from historically underperforming areas to new growth initiatives. Third, they leveraged assets in brand, customer service, and distribution to develop new growth opportunities. Fourth, they not only digitalized the customer experience and processes but also used technology to identify and create entirely new business models. And finally, they enabled organization-wide innovation that became ubiquitous.

The characteristics that Innosight uncovered in these organizations are similar to my description of the system of transformation. My system requires foundations of vision and strategy, business processes evaluated on a consistent basis, a continuous improvement framework like UnCLE, and people committed to promoting change through their participation and effort. And it is very important that the system has a leader who can identify and communicate the external opportunities, threats, or trends that affect transformation.

To test this assumption, I selected four Innosight-recognized organizations (one each in digital transformation, climate change, fintech, and health care) and summarized their transformation through the UnCLE framework to demonstrate how continuous improvement may have been integral to their transformation. The companies—Netflix, Ørsted, DBS Bank, and Philips—were selected based not on their respective rankings but on the extent of the disruption they encountered, the nature of their responses, and the gains pre- and post-transformation.

Netflix (Digital Transformation)

Netflix is number one among Innosight's Transformation 20. When Marc Randolph and Reed Hastings started the company in 1997, Netflix rented DVDs and video games through a subscription-based business model. In 2007, as a consequence of rapid developments in technology, Netflix started including streaming services to provide subscribers with an option that would reduce the costs of rentals and provide instant access to content.

Identify a Cause for Action

In 2013, Netflix found itself on an increasingly crowded stage of streaming providers such as Hulu Plus and Amazon Prime Video, with Apple TV Plus and Disney Plus waiting in the wings. Brandon Katz reports in the New York Observer that Netflix feared the company had peaked and might eventually succumb to its competitors. Hastings then released an 11-page memo to employees and investors that detailed a mission to move from just distributing content digitally to becoming a producer of original content that could win Emmys and Oscars.

Identify the Strategies and Tactics that Address the Cause

According to Mallika Rangaiah in *Analytic Steps*, Netflix approached the goal of providing original content in many ways. Foremost, it built alliances with a wide range of movie professionals to acquire, produce, and license material. It assembled actors, filmmakers, writers, and even animators to produce original shows based on data about what and whom viewers may enjoy watching. As a result, Netflix invested $100 million in *House of Cards*. To make access to content more readily available, the company built alliances with smart TV manufacturers LG and Sony, video game makers Microsoft (Xbox) and Sony (PlayStation), and streaming device producers Apple TV, Amazon Firestick, and Roku.

Netflix continued to enhance its value proposition for customers. The single fee for the subscriber and a restricted number of relatives and friends provided unlimited access to all content. The company improved its digital platform to enhance the viewer experience and began to recommend content using a detailed tagging system. For example, if the user watched a film in the thriller genre, comparable films in that category were suggested. This approach is based on the assumption that the viewer will watch similar shows in the future. Netflix also enhanced the customer experience by introducing thumbnails to maximize selection and by observing viewer patterns to predict bandwidth, optimize streaming quality at particular times, and produce content based on customers' preferences.

Through digital marketing, Netflix sought to increase viewer consumption of original content and boost brand image, including presenting itself as a progressive enterprise bringing change to the world. Social media, email, and interactive content continue to be important tools for promoting content that reflects the preference and diversity of its consumer base.

Measure Success against Internal Expectations and External Norms and Standards, then Build Upon the Outcomes

In 2018, Netflix's original content accounted for 37 percent of its streams, up from 14 percent in 2017. The company released 88 percent more original programming in 2018 than it did during 2017. Underlying these results are the outcomes experienced by Netflix during the five-year period following the decision to introduce original programming in 2013.

First, Netflix escalated the use of digital analytics to create a popular customer-friendly experience accentuated by enhanced streaming. Next, it increased member subscriptions from 34 million to 167 million. At the time of this writing, the company has nearly 193 million subscriptions worldwide. These numbers surpass its rival Amazon Prime, which provides its 150 million members with access to selected videos while charging an additional fee for premium content. Next in line as a competitor is Hulu Plus, which today has 30 million subscribers.

From 2013 to 2018, Netflix's revenue increased from $3.6 billion to $15.8 billion. When the company began its streaming services in 2007, its earnings were $997 million.

Introduce the Next Wave of Organizational Refinements and Innovations

According to a post on *Business Strategy Hub*, Netflix has become the most successful entertainment company of all time. It has converted its business model many times in response to internal requirements and external drivers of change. Through a successful startup and integration of rapid changes in technology, Netflix has improved its core business model—leading to more subscribers, especially since making the decision in 2013 to generate its own content.

But even with this success, Netflix continues to face challenges from the growing number of companies competing for distributed content. In 2018, its two most streamed shows in the United States were *Friends* and *The Office*, but these were acquired for distribution by HBO Max in 2020 and NBCUniversal in 2021, respectively.

Netflix has been preparing for the influx of competition from media conglomerates for years, according to Dana Feldman in *Forbes*. This is why Netflix spent $12 billion in 2018 building its library of original films and series, an 88 percent increase over 2017. The company has figured out that it must produce even more content at the highest quality in the future to retain and gain subscribers. For example, approximately 13 percent of lapsed Netflix subscribers re-enlisted when the third season of *Stranger Things*, one of its most popular series, was announced.

Netflix must also continue to capitalize on brand awareness. Most viewers of streaming content know Netflix. Feldman reports that it is the one video service that a vast majority of subscribers say they would not eliminate. Their selection far outpaces the next two choices, YouTube and cable TV.

One reason that Netflix is so popular is its ease of use—but beneath this simplicity is the company's very sophisticated, pioneering technology platform that makes downloading easy, eliminates buffering, and provides personalized messages. While these innovations were once groundbreaking, there is no guarantee that they will continue to distinguish Netflix from current and emerging providers.

Netflix's earnings for 2020 are expected to top $17 billion, outperforming its competition by a wide margin, thanks in part to the 12 million new viewers worldwide who subscribed at the onset of COVID-19. However, just a year earlier, its stock fell by 5 percent, adding to its overall debt of $12 billion.

Netflix needs to strengthen its financial model by first and foremost growing and retaining its customer base. In addition, bundling has been proposed as a revenue source. The idea is that Netflix, as a stand-alone streaming provider, needs to connect viewers to other services. For example, Apple TV Plus believes its content will help sell more iPhones. So far, Netflix has avoided advertising as a revenue source, which Feldman believes could help onboard more subscribers at a reduced rate. And because of the quality of Netflix productions, he believes nearly everyone would then upgrade to an upsell subscriber tier without commercials.

Another way to increase revenue is to continue diversifying original content. Katz believes that expanding interactive video, along with animated and young adult shows, could be lucrative. This would expand what is already a sweet spot, since 60 percent of Netflix's global audience is families with children.

Ørsted (Climate Change)

Ørsted is listed seventh among Innosight's Transformation 20 and is the highest-ranked European firm. Ørsted, as it came to be known in 2012, began in 1972 as Danish Oil and Natural Gas (DONG), a state-owned energy business specializing in building coal-fired power plants and sea-bound oil and gas rigs throughout Europe. In 1991, the firm began experimenting with offshore wind as a power source and constructed its first wind farm off the coast of Denmark, with 11 turbines producing 5 megawatts of power. Andrew Blum, in his post "How the Danish Energy Giant Plans to Revolutionize the U.S. Grid," contends that this was little more than a demonstration project, since DONG continued to focus on building up Denmark's oil and gas exploration capabilities in the North Sea.

Identify a Cause for Action

DONG's increased focus on green energy as a business model started in 2000, when Denmark and the United Kingdom expanded their commitment to climate change and turned attention to low-carbon wind power. This action came as the EU set its first carbon reduction goals in response to rising greenhouse gas emissions and warnings from scientists to break the trend. Denmark and the United Kingdom also experienced growing concern about their dependence on Russia for natural gas since Russia was involved at the time in the Second Chechen War, which both countries opposed.

In response to the concerns and actions of its two most important customers, DONG erected 80 two-megawatt turbines in the North Sea in 2002 to complement its oil production facilities there. By 2010, DONG was installing hundreds of turbines at a time, producing gigawatts of carbon-free power.

Despite this progress and commitment, S&P downgraded DONG's credit rating to a negative, raising the cost of the considerable debt it had incurred as a result of investing in green energy production. The financial predicament was worsened as global overproduction sent gas prices plunging 90 percent. At the same time, the company fired its chief executive over irregularities in employee contracts.

Identify the Strategies and Tactics that Address the Cause

It was during this period in 2012 that Ørsted's board of directors hired Henrik Poulsen, the former head of LEGO. Poulsen assessed 12 different lines of business, divested eight, and used the proceeds to reduce debt and defray the cost of building and running offshore wind farms while achieving scale in the market. He continued the company's "85/15 strategy," which would reverse the ratio of the company's business in favor of renewable energy: from 85 percent in fossil fuels and 15 percent in renewables in 2009 to 85 percent in renewables and 15 percent in fossil fuels by 2040. This transformation occurred in less than a decade. In recognition of this achievement and the dramatic shift to green energy, the company's name was changed in 2017 to honor 19th-Century Danish physicist Hans Christian Ørsted, who discovered electromagnetism.

In 2018, Poulsen announced plans to invest $30 billion in speeding up green energy to keep global warming within 1.5°C by 2030. This announcement was in concert with the company's seminal report "Taking Action to Stay within 1.5°C," which outlined actions such as cutting carbon emissions by half in accordance with the 2016 Paris Agreement and undertaking rapid reductions thereafter to achieve a balance between greenhouse gas emissions and removals in the second half of the century.

Measure Success against Internal Expectations and External Norms and Standards, then Build Upon the Outcomes

Over the last 10 years, Ørsted has dissolved its fossil fuel business, and now it focuses almost entirely on renewables. This commitment has paid off—in 2011, the company's annual revenue was $9.1 billion, and in 2018, it increased to nearly $11.8 billion. Once 80-percent-owned by the Danish government, Ørsted had an IPO in 2016 that was one of the year's largest.

Ørsted is now one of the largest green energy companies in the world. In 2018, it was ranked 70th by the Corporate Knights Global Index of most sustainable corporations; in 2019, it rose to fourth, and in 2020, it achieved first place.

In addition to its North Sea wind farms, Ørsted has built 6.8 gigawatts of offshore wind operations globally, leading the world (excluding mainland China) with 30 percent of the total. Operations totaling another 4.3 gigawatts are under construction in North America and Taiwan, and financing has been closed for another 3.1 gigawatts. In the midst of this activity, Ørsted sparked a manufacturing boom. For instance, the giant blades and turbines it uses are made in factories along the North Sea. New forms of sea vessels were created to aid in the construction process, including jack-up ships that can be deployed to different locations quickly, specialized vessels that ferry workers and equipment, and service operation ships that serve as floating hotels for technicians and can move from one location to the next.

Introduce the Next Wave of Organizational Refinements and Innovations

Global greenhouse gas emissions have skyrocketed, warns John Parnell in *Green Tech Media*. Yet as a global community, we have not managed to break the trend of increasing emissions—which Poulsen calls the defining challenge of our time. The foundations for countering this predicament at the corporate level are in place at Ørsted. Following a dramatic shift from a business model focused on building oil and gas rigs and coal-fired plants, the company now concentrates solely on offshore wind farm technology and construction. With this shift emerged a vision for the future: to help create a world that runs entirely on green energy.

To attain this lofty ambition, Ørsted seeks to achieve carbon neutrality by 2025 to become the most sustainable energy company ever. Next, it plans to become the global leader in onshore wind, solar energy, and storage solutions. The company also seeks to decarbonize the supply chain by phasing out gas trading activities while increasing the amount of green power traded. And finally, it seeks to build green energy in a sustainable way to not only halt climate change but also to ignite economic growth and advance social development. On this latter point, Ørsted has invested heavily in a public relations campaign depicting sustainability as a moral imperative and good business practice, since more investors and customers are seeking out environmentally sustainable companies.

On June 15, 2020, Poulsen announced his resignation as CEO of Ørsted, effective January 31, 2021. His tenure was highlighted by the emergence of what Parnell calls an offshore powerhouse, with an unrivaled pipeline of wind projects around the world and growing energy trading capabilities. Since the IPO in 2016, Ørsted shares have surged 220 percent.

It would appear, then, that the company's future is bright. However, there are a few areas where improvements might be necessary. The first is the need to amass long-term data on the effects of wind strength. In 2019, the absence of such data caused the company to underestimate the decrease in the speed of wind as it approaches wind farms and turbines. This resulted in overestimating the amount of time that turbines are generating electricity—a miscalculation that led to significant revenue losses. A second concern is the company's inability to compete with richer, larger companies that are investing in renewable energy, like BP and Royal Dutch Shell. This is tied to the final concern: the company's accumulation of debt to finance its expansion. According to Leslie Hook in the *Financial Times*, this strategy is dangerous, especially when demand for energy is low, as it was globally during the COVID-19 pandemic.

DBS Bank (Financial Technology)

At number 10 among the Transformation 20 is DBS, established in 1968 by the government of Singapore as Development Bank of Singapore Limited. Its founding represented an effort by the island nation, under the auspices of its economic development board, to upgrade and fund industrialization and attract foreign investments. DBS is included in the Transformation 20 as an example of conversion from a traditional regional bank into a global digital platform company specializing in financial services. Now DBS is the largest bank in Southeast Asia, with a solid digital footprint across the globe.

Identify a Cause for Action

DBS was not always an international leader in the fintech industry. In 2009, it had the lowest ratings of any bank in Singapore. This was due, in part, to unacceptable service that penetrated every aspect of the enterprise, from customer interactions to loan approvals and account openings.

The bank was not viewed as a trusted partner, and it suffered a 22-percent final quarter revenue loss compared to the previous calendar year.

This standing was hardly representative of Singapore's intended movement toward greater globalization. The downward trend was occurring even as virtual banking services were emerging in Europe, especially the United Kingdom. At that moment, DBS was not prepared to enter the era of smart banking.

Identify the Strategies and Tactics that Address the Cause

During that time, Piyush Gupta was hired to lead the struggling company. Before considering digitalization, Gupta instituted a new corporate strategy to strengthen the bank's relationship with its existing customer base. The approach centered on the concept of "Asian-ness," with an emphasis on values abbreviated as RED: respectful, easy to deal with, and dependable. RED became the focus for process improvement to eliminate wasted customer time, known in DBS parlance as the "customer hour."

This led to a shift to a more customer-centered approach, which recognized the importance of banking to complement daily life. DBS then began expanding its digital footprint to accommodate this sentiment. It moved from thinking like a bank to acting like a tech company; its digital transformation was fueled by user-friendly application programming interfaces (APIs) and accentuated by flexible architecture, automated processes, and analytics integration. These changes were designed to create a sophisticated, all-encompassing digital ecosystem that honors the customer journey. According to Jason Bloomberg in *Forbes*, the new system allowed DBS to make the business of banking invisible, an approach that the bank calls "Live More, Bank Less."

Gupta believes the multisided digital approach at DBS is wired to respond flexibly to disruption, allowing the bank to move ahead of competitors. Among these moves was the creation of Digibank in India—an entirely mobile-centric banking service with no physical branches and, consequently, a tiny fraction of the back-office staff that a conventional bank normally requires.

DBS also expended considerable time and effort to change the culture of the organization from a focus on conventional approaches to an emphasis on digital transformation. Teams were established to teach and instill innovation across the organization. Internal training programs provided the freedom and agility for 26,000 employees to adopt a startup mentality. Activities centered on design thinking, data analytics, and "hackathons" as a way to integrate employee skills and technology to transform the culture and enhance the customer experience. KPIs were set around innovation targets. The new culture helped customers become more trusting. They could now expect DBS to deliver services quickly and efficiently, especially in the virtual world where customers now spend much of their time.

Measure Success against Internal Expectations and External Norms and Standards, then Build Upon the Outcomes

Today, DBS is a multinational organization recognized for its transition from a bank to a tech company specializing in financial services. This conversion required creating an innovative digital platform to simplify the customer and employee journeys, support data-driven decision-making, and transform the company culture.

As a consequence, Seng Wei Keng reports in "DBS: On Becoming the Wizard of Digital Transformation" that the organization has experienced efficiencies by attracting customers that generate three times as much income, maintain higher loan and deposit balances, and cost up to 57 percent less to acquire than customers who visit a physical branch. Forty-eight percent of its customer base is on digital platforms, and some 96 percent of its new account openings are done online. Digital customers are doing 30 percent more transactions in both volume and value. They also make 16 times more self-service transactions and achieve a 27 percent return on equity, in contrast to 19 percent for traditional customers.

Following its record decline in 2009, DBS' annual revenue rose to $7.6 billion two years later. By 2018, it was nearly $13.4 billion. This strong capital position and superior credit ratings by S&P and Moody's helped the company earn multiple awards from *Global Finance, Euromoney,* and *The Banker.*

Introduce the Next Wave of Organizational Refinements and Innovations

As its journey continues, DBS looks to the tech giants in Silicon Valley as an example of experimentation at scale to determine how customers behave in real time. According to Gupta, this data will be fundamental to further transformation—transformation that has been accelerated by COVID-19.

This idea is shared by Ida Morris, who notes in "5 Trends that Will Define the Future of Fintech in 2020" that the coronavirus is fueling a 72-percent rise in fintech apps as the desire for contactless banking intensifies. Mobile payment technology is expected to grow by 36 percent over the next five years, especially within the millennial and Gen Z populations, who are already accustomed to using such technologies. This growth coincides with the expanded use of secure biometric measures, such as fingerprint and facial scanning and voice recognition, which are expected to perform better and faster in the highly anticipated 5G environment.

In an interview with Jason Li and Joydeep Sengupta of McKinsey & Company, Gupta says that in order to compete in the growing fintech sector, DBS must remain committed to improvements that address customer needs with efficiency, reliability, and personalization. He says this is what separates DBS from similar financial institutions but that it requires an ongoing investment in digital transformation. The company already has implemented many innovations, including biometric screening. According to Nikhar Aggarwal in "Reinventing Banking: A Look at DBS Bank's Digital Transformation Journey," DBS is moving beyond customer interfaces that use the Internet to a system that supports individualized services, utilizes cloud capabilities, introduces more APIs, and leverages automation—all in a culture in which exploration is critical and innovation, in response to digital disruption, is embraced and celebrated. DBS is also leveraging its strengths to make a social impact designed to advance sustainability and improve financial inclusion among the "underbanked."

Despite the upbeat outlook, DBS must be prepared to address challenges along with other fintechs. First, while these companies combine finance and technology to improve efficiency and customer satisfaction, they are still banks with fundamental risks, especially during an economic downturn. Consequently, many countries are strengthening regulations to mitigate the dangers that are particularly associated with startups. Next, although the financial distribution channels are new, the business model is not. Traditional banks can replicate many of the fintech services and can commit more resources to the process. Large conventional banks such as J.P. Morgan are already seeking to compete in the fintech arena by applying innovations like blockchain to improve processes and transactions and strengthen customer relations. Finally, data exposure and the cybersecurity practices to mitigate them present additional concerns. This is particularly true among most fintech companies because they permit consumers to control multiple accounts on a single platform. DBS may somewhat mitigate this risk by maintaining both digital and physical platforms.

Philips (Health Care)

Our final case study, at number 20 in the Transformation 20, is Philips, which was founded in 1891 by Frederik Philips to make carbon filament lamps. Over 129 years, the company experimented with and achieved innovations in X-ray radiation and radio reception, appliance and television production, audio technology (such as the audio cassette and audio disc), and imaging (leading to the DVD, for example).

In 1990, the company began capitalizing on its success in imaging to adopt a new customer-centric approach to health care. This approach was aimed at making medical systems easier to use by clinicians and more comfortable for patients. In 2002, Philips introduced the Ambient Experience, which essentially institutionalized its focus on health care among its other businesses, including electronics and lighting.

Identify a Cause for Action

Amid this transformation, Philips experienced a financial slump, partly because of its divergent business interests. In particular, a third-quarter decline of 85 percent in 2011 resulted in layoffs of 4,500 employees. At the same moment, health care organizations worldwide were facing unprecedented challenges, including the need to reduce cost structures by adopting affordable equipment and digital strategies. If Philips hoped to compete in this space, a major restructuring was inevitable.

Identify the Strategies and Tactics that Address the Cause

During this time, Philips appointed Frans van Houten, who had joined the company in 1986, as its new CEO. Van Houten's first act was to launch Accelerate, a program intended to revitalize and transform Philips into a health technology company through targeted divestments, acquisitions, investments, and organic business development that included an emphasis on recycling.

In concert with this movement, Philips divested its television, audio, and video manufacturing interests between 2011 and 2014. The company immediately began strengthening its health care business through a series of acquisitions, beginning with the Volcano Corporation in 2015, to improve its position in non-invasive surgery and imaging. In 2017, it acquired Spectranetics, a manufacturer of devices to treat heart disease, to expand its image-guided therapy business.

That same year, Philips launched a health technology venture fund to invest in companies such as Mytonomy and DEARhealth, seeking to improve the patient experience and outcomes while reducing costs. As further evidence of its desire to establish an independent health technology business, Philips separated its lighting division in 2016 to create Philips Lighting, which was renamed Signify in 2018 but which continues to produce and market Phillips-branded products.

Van Houten also introduced the idea of "circular economy" as a competitive advantage. This concept entails establishing leasing relationships, restoring and upgrading returned equipment, and sending the equipment to another customer. This was an important strategy to position the company to supply expensive equipment more affordably to customers who, as they factored both price and conservation into their buying decisions, realized that a refurbished machine was as dependable as a new one.

The final key to van Houten's ambitious plan was motivating employees to understand the significance of health technology to the organization since transformation hinged on abolishing long-standing silos. Van Houten believed that multidisciplinary teamwork, not individual effort, would speed transformation, promote technological innovation, and bring products to market in a short time.

Measure Success against Internal Expectations and External Norms and Standards, then Build Upon the Outcomes

In a review of Philips, crowd-sourced content service Seeking Alpha reports that under van Houten's leadership, the company transformed from a sprawling conglomerate that did just about everything into an organization that is focused on providing comprehensive and innovative solutions—not merely products—to the health care industry in three areas.

The first area focuses on precision diagnosis and treatment using image-guided, minimally invasive procedures. The next is connected care for patients using advanced analytics and workflow to optimize patient care, both inside and outside the hospital. The final area is personal health, emphasizing healthy living and preventative care. The portion of the business represented by these areas grew from 50 percent in 2011 to 98 percent in 2019. While revenues shrank from $31 billion in 2014 to $24.3 billion in 2018, profit margins for the period moved from 2 to 6 percent. Net income for the period surged by 165 percent.

This transformation has helped the company emerge as one of three medical imaging industry leaders that together account for 70 percent of sales worldwide. Philips, at 18 percent, is joined by Siemens with a 32 percent share and General Electric with 20 percent. Among its competitors, Philips is most like Siemens with respect to digital innovation and strategic partnerships with customers. However, Philips is in a better position financially to acquire companies that can complete its transition to an enterprise that is focused entirely on health technology. Its potential for margin improvements is also significant when compared to Siemens. Philips is further differentiated from its competitor by innovative technology platforms for image-guided therapy and ultrasound.

Philips has delivered on its commitment to its circular economy initiative. It created the Circular Products and Solutions unit, whose goal is to improve patient outcomes, provide better value, and help secure access to high-quality technology. It seeks all this while reducing environmental impact and minimizing natural resource consumption and its carbon footprint. In 2019, the unit accounted for 13 percent of gross revenue.

As indicated, sustainability is now key to the company's transformation. Through its "Healthy People, Sustainable Planet" program, Philips is committed to becoming fully carbon neutral in its own operations. It now secures all its electricity from 100 percent renewable energy sources, and it strives to reduce carbon emissions across the company and its supply chain by 2025 to align with the 1.5°C global warming cap.

In an interview with Thomas Fleming and Markus Zils ("Toward a Circular Economy"), van Houten attributes Philips' achievements to the collaboration of its employees. For example, units no longer focus on producing specific products; rather, cross-functional teams are enlisted to concentrate on specific goals. Consequently, silos are broken down, empowering Philips to become a solutions company rather than primarily a product company. One example is Philips' response to the COVID-19 pandemic. The company created telehealth solutions to centrally monitor and manage patients in the hospital and at home. Simultaneously, it quadrupled production of hospital ventilators and other life-saving technologies, including diagnostic imaging systems.

Introduce the Next Wave of Organizational Refinements and Innovations

Health technology, especially in the medical imaging field in which Philips excels, is expected to continue as a growth industry whose space is an entrenched oligopoly. This technology is used to dispense prevention, intervention, and therapeutic services, and as such, it touches every area of health care and serves not only as a software/data platform for operations but also as a profit center for most organizations. This is why Philips will continue to expand and fortify its customer base through the availability of new and recycled equipment as it works to strengthen health outcomes, improve the patient and staff experience, and lower the cost of care.

In a 2019 letter to stakeholders, van Houten reinforces these ideals, writing that Philips will remain committed to meeting customers' needs through innovation, compelling solutions, and improvements in the supply chain to boost productivity. This entails strengthening internal processes through digitalization. Philips also seeks to further fortify its core businesses, especially Image Guided Therapy, through smart devices. The planned divestiture of its Domestic Appliance Division, which is not considered a strategic fit for the future, will allow Philips to transition into a company focused entirely on health technology and will fund innovation and targeted acquisitions and partnerships to achieve this status.

But Philips faces challenges as it moves forward with its ambitious agenda, and these concerns are not unlike those of other health care enterprises. They generate uncertainty, but they also present opportunities to create innovative responses for both the short and long terms—responses that can result in substantially reduced costs while providing higher quality and better outcomes that help people live longer, healthier, and more active lifestyles.

The fate of the Affordable Care Act in the hands of the U.S. Supreme Court is one of the immediate challenges. Whether the act is repealed or upheld, either decision can have a profound impact on insurance coverage and health care delivery. Another area to be dealt with is burdensome government regulations and standards, including those associated with the Health Insurance Portability and Accountability Act (HIPAA).

According to Prinsez Teel in *Becker's Hospital Review*, as the intersection of medicine and technology grows, it will create more consumer-centered, integrated health care systems, such as a shift from traditional office visits toward virtual office visits. Companies need to be ahead of this inevitability. One answer subscribed to by Philips and supported by Shubham Singhal in

"Seven Healthcare Industry Trends to Watch in 2020" can be found in mergers, acquisitions, and investments that allow the adoption of new technology business models and refinement of existing ones. As the use of technology escalates, cybersecurity measures are mandatory, since health care records in particular are subjects of ransomware invasions by criminals who are becoming increasingly smarter and more persistent.

The value of medications to a quality life is unquestioned but challenging. For example, approval by insurers for the use of specialty drugs in treating complex and rare diseases is up by 9.4 percent. But these drugs, unfortunately, cost 50 times more than traditional drugs. Prescriptions for brand-name drugs are also expensive, with costs increasing by 57 percent from 2014 to 2019. During the same time, generic drug prices actually dropped by 35 percent.

COVID-19 is sure to have a long-term effect on health care. Organizations have yet to determine the true length of the recovery period or when to expect a return to normal in areas such as office appointments, elective and outpatient surgeries, and emergency room visits. Regardless, a certain volume of telehealth and remote work will continue. Unfortunately, there will be casualties among organizations based on disparities in financial stability that were evident before the pandemic.

Like the leaders of transformation described earlier, the leaders of these Transformation 20 companies responded to change strategically by recognizing disruptors in the market and deliberately responding to them. Even more recent drivers of change, such as sustainability, COVID-19, and racial and economic equity, were factored into their responses. A common theme among the companies is that changes took considerable time to play out—on average five years. It would appear, then, that at the heart of their strategic transformation is continuous improvement. They adapted to disruptive change while also repositioning core businesses and gradually instituting new growth. It also appears that the transformation was aided by a framework, like UnCLE, that permitted identifying an opportunity for change, developing the responses, measuring the results, and sustaining and building on the outcomes in anticipation of the next opportunity for change.

Lagniappe

A little something extra

The year 2020 will be remembered as one of the most disruptive in our nation's recent history. A terrifying and divisive pandemic, unprecedented racial unrest, and a contentious presidential election will all shape American society for years to come. Add to this the already pervasive effects of technology, climate change, and global affairs, like the ongoing volatility in the Middle East and friction with China and Russia, and we begin to understand the immense challenges in daily life and the workplace that are projected for the future.

Fortunately, challenges like these provide an opportunity to reaffirm our organizations' core foundations—values, vision, culture, and strategy—and a chance to double down on the crucial role of the workforce in a troubling environment. But given the enormity of these current drivers of change, more effective organizational development and leadership approaches and better change strategies will be required.

Throughout *Capturing Change*, I have attempted to show that traditional change management activities cannot support the type of response we need to address current and future disruptors. This response must be immediate but at the same time gradual and deliberate. We will need approaches in which leaders effectively embed the possible "new normals" into change initiatives *and* everyday operations. Even in the midst of downright uncertainty, leaders must have confidence that their approaches are reliable when implemented properly.

In "How Businesses Can Turn Crises to Their Advantage," Deepankar Sanwalka says that such approaches create "disruption-ready" organizations, which emerge stronger after turning crisis into advantage. I prefer to call these organizations systems of transformation, led by leaders of transformation. In these organizations, disruption is not just anticipated but welcomed, because it creates an opportunity to build on achievements and explore and experience new growth opportunities. Such organizations, according to Jeroen Kraaijenbrink in *Forbes*, do not consider just temporary fixes in the face of disruption but view the moment as a chance to equip the organization for the future.

One need look no further than the Innosight Transformation 20 organizations for examples of these qualities. In each case, the organization confronted an external foe that required both immediate and measured solutions. Most of the companies hired new CEOs, each of whom conducted a thorough analysis and used it to create a vision of where the organization could gain an advantage. Short- and long-term actions followed for enacting the vision. The CEOs applied measures throughout their processes to determine if the actions and outcomes could move the organizations to the next level and toward transformation. In the throes of these activities, corrective actions were taken when warranted. Challenges such as socioeconomic disruption, workplace diversity, and climate change were not ignored but incorporated as strategic priorities to benefit employee engagement, the organization's image, its social action agenda, and the bottom line.

The Transformation 20 organizations represent an important premise of *Capturing Change*: that continuous improvement is a more efficient approach than change management to guide transformation. It is deliberate yet allows an immediate response to disruption, particularly when good business processes and practices exist. As a result, leaders of transformation must fully understand the benefits of continuous improvement to achieve ongoing and enduring change and to create and operate systems of transformation.

While developing these systems is tough, sustaining them is even more daunting. I have already alluded to the pitfalls, especially the downside of not engaging people. Without the necessary human support, including what John Kotter terms a "guiding coalition," change is doomed, and even routine work is at risk.

Gaining and keeping support is aided by the ability to anticipate drivers of change, to determine the impact they will have on the organization, and to identify and communicate the response. This requires being knowledgeable about the convergence of types of change—developmental, transitional, and transformational—with underlying process improvement through the PDCA cycle. This is all guided by vision and strategy and is the essence of continuous improvement focused on ongoing operations that incorporate and support change as an integral part of organizational development. UnCLE is the ideal tool for organizing this effort.

Once again, this responsibility is carried out in a manner that engages people at a meaningful and productive level. This engagement is a crucial aspect of continuous improvement. And as leaders of transformation undertake this work, they will not only benefit individually but will also become a model for everyone in their spheres of influence.

I believe the approach represented in *Capturing Change* reflects the next generation of leading and consulting beyond change management. But becoming a leader of transformation requires you to pursue your own learning and development—changing your mindset, altering your behaviors, and evolving your leadership or consulting style and approaches. It means expanding your thinking about process and your repertoire for designing and facilitating the complexities of transformation. It demands taking a stand for the personal change required of leaders and within the workforce.

I believe that by consciously capturing change, leaders of transformation can effectively catch lightning in a bottle. As a leader of transformation, you can use ongoing change as a catalyst for overcoming the challenges—whether human, technical, or environmental—that coincide with organizational advancement. Rather than fearing the storms, you can create a future that allows our organizations and society to thrive.

References

Nikhar Aggarwal. "Reinventing Banking: A Look at DBS Bank's Digital Transformation Journey." Retrieved from https://cio.economictimes.indiatimes.com/news/strategy-and-management/reinventing-banking-a-look-at-dbs-banks-digital-transformation-journey/77754858

Kamran Akbarzadeh. *Leadership Soup: A Healthy Yet Tasty Recipe for Living and Leading with Purpose.* Bloomington, MN: Xlibris Corporation, 2011.

David Anderson. "Managing Global Risk in a Changing World." Leaders, July 2017.

Dean Anderson and Linda Ackerman Anderson. *Beyond Change Management. How to Achieve Breakthrough Results through Conscious Change Leadership.* Second Edition. San Francisco, CA: Pfeiffer, 2010.

John Anderson, Manus Rungtusanatham, and Roger Schroeder. "A Theory of Quality Management Underlying the Deming Management Method." *Academy of Management Review*, 19(3), 1994.

Linda Ackerman Anderson and Dean Anderson. *The Change Leader's Roadmap. How to Navigate your Organization's Transformation.* Second edition. San Francisco, CA: Pfeiffer, 2010.

Linda Ackerman Anderson and Dean Anderson. *Awake at the Wheel: Moving Beyond Change Management to Conscious Change Leadership.* Retrieved from https://changeleadersnetwork.com/free-resources/awake-at-the-wheel-moving-beyond-change-management-to-conscious-change-leadership

Ron Ashkenas. "It's Time to Rethink Continuous Improvement." Retrieved from https://www.wikihow.com/Develop-a-Culture-of-Continuous-Improvement

Jaakko Aspara, Juha-Antti Lamberg, Arjo Laukia, and Henrikki Tikkanen. "Corporate Business Model Transformation and Inter-Organizational Cognition: The Case of Nokia." *Long Range Planning*, 46(6), 2013.

Mark Avallone. "The Economic Impacts of Recent Hurricanes and Tax Reform." *Forbes*, October 12, 2017.

Jesse Barfield, Caroline Fisher, Jing Li, and Rajiv Mehta. "Retesting a Model of the Deming Management Method." *Total Quality Management and Business Excellence*, 16(3), 2005.

Jason Bloomberg. "How DBS Bank Became the Best Digital Bank in the World by Becoming Invisible." *Forbes*, December 23, 2016

Andrew Blum. "How the Danish Energy Giant Plans to Revolutionize the US Grid." Retrieved from https://www.protocol.com/wind-massachusetts-orsted-energy

Orrin Broberg. "Eight Ways Technology is Changing Business." Retrieved from https://www.gomodus.com/blog/eight-ways-technology-changing-business

Bob Bryan and Joe Ciolli. "Here's How the Newly Passed GOP Tax Bill Will Impact the Economy, Businesses, the Deficit, and Your Wallet." *Business Insider*, December 20, 2017.

Bernard Burnes. *Managing Change. Seventh Edition.* London, England: Pearson, 2018.

Business Strategy Hub. "Netflix Business Model (2020): How Does Netflix Make Money?" Retrieved from https://bstrategyhub.com/netflix-business-model-how-does-netflix-make-money/

Bill Carmody. "3 Reasons Celebrating Your Many Accomplishments Is Critical to your Success." Retrieved from https://www.inc.com/bill-carmody/3-reasons-celebrating-your-many-accomplishments-is-critical-to-your-success.html

Jeaw-Mei Chen, Mein-Woei Suen, Mei-Jong Lin, and Fu-An Shieh. "Organizational Change and Development." Retrieved from https://www.academia.edu/14737325/Organizational_Change_and_Development

Roger Cheng. "5G is Almost a Reality. Here's What It'll Really Feel Like." Retrieved from https://intellecy.com/5g-is-almost-a-reality-heres-what-itll-really-feel-like

Rohit Chopra and Juan Mier. "Profitability Trends in Emerging Markets Setting the Stage for Active Management." Retrieved from https://www.lazardassetmanagement.com/docs/sp0/19421/ProfitabilityTrendsInEmergingMarkets-_LazardResearch.pdf

Joseph Chris. "Seven Howard Schultz Leadership Style Principles." Retrieved from https://www.josephchris.com/7-howard-schultz-leadership-style-principles

Faye Chua. "Drivers of Change in the U.S." Association of Chartered Certified Accountants, February 2013.

Don Clifton. CliftonStrengths *Strengthsfinder 360*. Retrieved from https://www.insyte360.com/strengthsfinder/

Toby Cosgrove. *The Cleveland Clinic Way: Lessons in Excellence from One of the World's Leading Health Care Organizations*. New York, NY: McGraw-Hill Education, 2014.

Diane Coutu. "Putting Leaders on the Couch." *Harvard Business Review on the Mind of the Leader*. Cambridge, Massachusetts: Harvard Business School Publishing Corporation, 2005.

Barry Dalal-Clayton and Stephen Bass. "Sustainable Development through Regional Economic Strategies." Retrieved from https://rozitoxuhafe.inksster.icu/sustainable-development-through-regional-economic-strategies-book-1455om.php#

Marc Davis. "Government Regulations: Do they Help Businesses?" *Investopedia*, July 23, 2020.

John DiJulius. *The Customer Service Revolution*. Cleveland, OH: The Dijulius Group, 2015.

DiversityInc. "The 2020 DiversityInc Top 50 Companies for Diversity." Retrieved from https://www.diversityinc.com/the-2020-top-50-diversityinc/

Elizabeth Douglas. "How to Develop a Culture of Continuous Improvement." Retrieved from https://www.wikihow.com/Develop-a-Culture-of-Continuous-Improvement

Dana Feldman. "The Future of Netflix: Is it Really as Doom and Gloom as People are Saying." *Forbes*, July 15, 2019.

Thomas Fleming and Markus Zils. "Toward a Circular Economy: Philips CEO Frans van Houten." Retrieved from https://www.mckinsey.com/business-functions/sustainability/our-insights/toward-a-circular-economy-philips-ceo-frans-van-houten

Heather Fork. "What are Your Natural Gifts? Is your Job Making the Most of Them?" *Doctors Crossing*, January 21, 2012.

David Garvin. "Building a Learning Organization." *Harvard Business Review*, July–August 1993.

Patrick Gleeson. "Factors that May Cause Change in an Organization." Retrieved from https://smallbusiness.chron.com/factors-may-cause-change-organization-203.html

Daniel Goleman. "What Makes a Leader?" In *Harvard Business Review* on the Mind of the Leader. Cambridge, Massachusetts: Harvard Business School Publishing Corporation, 2005.

Carol Kinsey Gorman. "8 tips for Collaborative Leadership." *Forbes*, February 13, 2014.

John Hall. "7 Ways to Identify and Evolve with Industry Trends." Retrieved from https://www.inc.com/john-hall/7-ways-to-identify-and-evolve-with-industry-trends.html

James Harrington, Frank Voehl, and Christopher Voehl. "Model for Sustainable Change." *PMI White Papers*, 2015.

Witold Henisz and Bennet Zelner. "The Strategic Organization of Political Risk and Opportunities." *Strategic Organization*, 1(4), 2003.

Jefferey Hiatt and Timothy Creasey. Change Management: *The People Side of Change*. Loveland, CO: Prosci, Inc., 2012.

Phil Higson and Anthony Sturgess. *Uncommon Leadership: How to Build a Competitive Advantage by Thinking Differently*. Philadelphia, PA: Kogan Page, 2014.

E.D. Hirsch. *Cultural Literacy: What Every American Needs to Know*. New York, NY: Vintage Press, 1988.

Leslie Hooks. "Orsted Completes World's Largest Offshore Wind Farm in Irish Sea. Retrieved from https://www.ft.com/content/4ff3e830-b162-11e8-8d14-6f049d06439c

Herminia Ibarra and Morten Hansen. "Are You a Collaborative Leader?" *Harvard Business Review*, July–August 2011.

Sinem Ikinci. "Organizational Change: Importance of Leadership Style and Training." *Management and Organizational Studies*, 1(2), 2014.

Masaaki Imai. Kaizen: *The Key to Japan's Competitive Success*. New York, NY: McGraw-Hill, 1986.

Innosight. "The Transformation 20." Retrieved from https://www.innosight.com/wp-content/uploads/2019/09/Innosight-Transformation-20-Final.pdf

Alex Johnson. *Change the Lapel Pin: Personalizing Leadership for Organizations and Communities*. Cleveland, OH: Smart Business Network, 2018.

Kanbanize.com. "Benefits of Continuous Improvement as a Business Strategy." Retrieved from https://kanbanize.com/blog/how-continuous-improvement-can-benefit-your-business/

Richard Kastenbaum. "Great Stores Are Still the Best Way to Make Consumers Love a Brand." *Forbes*, January 30, 2017.

Brandon Katz. "Netflix Needs Some New Tricks if it Wants to Stay on Top." Retrieved from: https://observer.com/2020/03/netflix-stock-compete-amazon-apple-disney-plus/

Joe Kelly. "Examples of Companies that Change Their Strategies." Retrieved from https://smallbusiness.chron.com/examples-companies-change-strategies-14307.html

Seng Wei Keng. "DBS: On Becoming the Wizard of Digital Transformation." Retrieved from https://www.fsisac.com/insights/dbs-becoming-the-wizard-of-digital-transformation

Randy Kiersz. "Trump Claims the Tax Bill Would Lead to a Huge Boost for Business Spending and Hiring—Executives aren't as Sure." *Business Insider*, November 17, 2017.

Andrew King, Dominic Johnson, and Mark Van Vugt. "The Origins and Evolution and Evolution of Leadership." *Current Biology*, October 2009.

Firas Kittaneh. "6 Growth Challenges Your Business Will Face (and How to Overcome Them)." Retrieved from https://www.inc.com/firas-kittaneh/6-growth-challenges-your-business-will-face-and-how-to-overcome-them.html

John Kotter. *Leading Change*. Boston, MA: Harvard Business Review Press, 2012.

KPMG. "Disruptive Trends: Geopolitics." Retrieved from https://home.kpmg/content/dam/kpmg/ie/pdf/2016/10/ie-aci-disruption-geopolitics.pdf

Jeroen Kraaijenbrink. "3 Reasons Why You Should Use This Crisis to Make a Change." *Forbes*, May 13, 2020.

Lisa Kudray and Brian Kleiner. "Global Trends in Managing Change." *Industrial Magazine*, 39(3), 1997.

Patrick Lencioni. *The advantage: Why organizational health trumps everything else in business*. San Francisco, CA: Jossey-Bass, 2012.

Shana Lenowitz. "From Projects to a $2.3 Billion Fortune: The Inspiring Rags to Riches Story of Starbucks CEO Howard Schultz." *Business Insider*, May 30, 2015.

Jason Li and Joydeep Sengupta. "Becoming More than a Bank: Digital Transformation at DBS." Retrieved from https://www.mckinsey.com/industries/financial-services/our-insights/banking-matters/becoming-more-than-a-bank-digital-transformation-at-dbs

Tero Lindholm. "Implementing SPI: Combining Business Process Improvement and System Development at Nokia." Retrieved from https://2019.eurospi.net/images/proceedings/EuroSPI1998-Proceedings.pdf

Kendall Lyman and Tony Daloisio. *Change the Way You Change: 5 Roles of Leaders Who Accelerate Business Performance*. Austin, TX: gbgpress, 2017.

Anna Mar. "Change Management vs. Continuous Improvement." Retrieved from https://management.simplicable.com/management/new/change-management-vs-continuous-improvement#:~:text=Change%20management%20focuses%20on%20the,focus%20on%20processes%20and%20products

Jack Marchewka. "An Application of the Deming Management Method for Information Technology Projects." *Journal of International Technology and Information Management*, 16(2), 2007.

Paris Martinez and Louise Matsakis. "Why it's Hard to Escape Amazon's Long Reach." Retrieved from https://amp.flipboard.com/@WIRED/why-it-s-hard-to-escape-amazon-s-long-reach/a-2AHCgssRTdak2q3HJVZGsw%3Aa%3A3089933-a8c5ebf587%2Fwired.com

John Mayer and Peter Salovey. "The Intelligence of Emotional Intelligence." *Intelligence*, October–December 1993.

David McCoy. "Process Improvement Projects On-Boarding & Off-Boarding." Retrieved from https://prezi.com/rkhjoixef0be/process-improvement-projects-on-boarding-off-boarding/

Heather McGowan. "How the Coronavirus Pandemic is Accelerating the Future of Work." *Forbes*, March 23, 2020.

McKinsey & Company. "Building Organizational Capabilities." Retrieved from https://www.mckinsey.com/~/media/McKinsey/Business%20Functions/Organization/Our%20Insights/Building%20organizational%20capabilities%20McKinsey%20Global%20Survey%20results/Building%20organizational%20capabilities%20McKinsey%20Global%20Survey%20results.pdf

McKinsey & Company. "The Four Building Blocks of Change." *McKinsey Quarterly*, April 11, 2006.

McKinsey & Company. "Enduring Ideas: The 7-S Framework." *McKinsey Quarterly*, March 1, 2008.

Debra Meyerson. "Radical Change, the Quiet Way." *On Change Management*. Cambridge, Massachusetts: Harvard Business School Publishing Corporation, 2011.

Lawrence Miller. *Getting to Lean—Transformational Change*. Sarasota, FL: Miller Management Press LLC, 2013.

Mind Tools. "Lewin's Change Management Model: Understanding the Three Stages of Change." Retrieved from https://www.mindtools.com/pages/article/newPPM_94.htm

Ida Morris. "5 Trends that Will Define the Future of Fintech in 2020." Retrieved from https://www.mni.com/blog/research/fintech-trends-2020/article_9674e574-7f25-11ea-bbb0-dba1d9f41807.html

Langdon Morris. "The Driving Forces of Change." Retrieved from https://innovationmanagement.se/2013/07/18/the-driving-forces-of-change/

Ben Mulholland. "8 Critical Change Management Models to Evolve and Survive." Retrieved from https://www.process.st/change-management-models/

Mike Myatt. "The Impact of Trends on Business." Retrieved from https://www.n2growth.com/does-your-business-capitalize-on-trends-or-do-trends-cannibalize-your-business/

Gonzalo Pangaro, Michael Cornelius, and Ernest Yeunge. "Volatility Driving Dispersion in Emerging Markets." Retrieved from https://www.troweprice.com/content/dam/ide/articles/pdfs/544839-volatility-driving-dispersion-in-emerging-markets.pdf

John Parnell. "Job Done: Ørsted CEO Poulsen Resigns from Global Offshore Wind Leader." Retrieved from https://www.greentechmedia.com/articles/read/orsted-ceo-poulsen-resigns#:~:text=%C3%98rsted%20CEO%20Henrik%20Poulsen%20has,general%20meeting%20in%20March%202021

Planview.com. "Business Process Improvement Guide." Retrieved from https://www.planview.com/fr/resources/guide/business-process-improvement/

Michael Porter. "How Competitive Forces Shape Strategy." *Harvard Business Review*, March 1979.

Mallika Rangaiah. "Using Data Handling and Digital Marketing to Maximize Customer Experience: A Netflix Case Study." Retrieved from https://www.analyticssteps.com/blogs/using-data-handling-and-digital-marketing-maximise-customer-experience-netflix-case-study

Martin Reeves and Johann Harnoss. "An Agenda for the Future of Global Business." *Harvard Business Review*, February 27, 2017.

Andy Rowsell-Jones and John Roberts. "Improving Business Processes." Retrieved from https://www.gartner.com/en/documents/967012/improving-business-processes

Megan Ruesink. "Top Corporate Mergers: The Good, the Bad & the Ugly." Retrieved from https://www.rasmussen.edu/degrees/business/blog/best-and-worst-corporate-mergers/

Manus Rungtusanatham, Cipriano Forza, Roberto Fillipini, and John Anderson. "A Replication of a Theory of Quality Management Underlying the Deming Management Method: Insights from an Italian Context." *Journal of Operations Management*, 17, 1998.

Deepankar Sanwalka. "How Businesses Can Turn Crises to Their Advantage." Retrieved from https://www.weforum.org/agenda/2019/10/how-to-manage-a-business-crisis/

Howard Schultz. *From the Ground Up: A Journey to Reimagine the Promise of America*. New York, NY: Random House, 2019.

Seeking Alpha. "Philips: High Margin of Safety and 10% IRR Make this Medical Imaging Play a Buy." Retrieved from https://seekingalpha.com/article/4323940-philips-high-margin-of-safety-and-10-irr-make-this-medical-imaging-play-buy

Jiseon Shin, Myeong-Gu Seo, Debra L. Shapiro, and Susan Taylor. "Maintaining "Employees' Commitment to Organizational Change: The Role of Leaders' Informational Justice and Transformational Leadership." *The Journal of Applied Behavioral Science*, 51(4), 2015.

Shubham Singhal. "Seven Healthcare Industry Trends to Watch in 2020." Retrieved from https://www.mckinsey.com/industries/healthcare-systems-and-services/our-insights/seven-healthcare-industry-trends-to-watch-in-2020

Christopher Smith. "Understanding Transformational Change Management." Retrieved from https://change.walkme.com/understanding-transformational-change-management/

Jimmy Smith. "Continuous Improvement: A Journey, not a Destination." *Peoria Magazine*, June 2012.

Jacqueline Stavros and Cheri Torres. *Conversations Worth Having: Using Appreciative Inquiry to Fuel Productive and Meaningful Engagement.* Oakland, CA: Berrett-Koehler Publishers, 2018.

Sara Stibitz. 2015. "How to Really Listen to Your Employees." *Harvard Business Review*, January 30, 2015.

Donald Sull. "Why Good Companies Go Bad." *Harvard Business Review.* July–August, 1999.

Prinsez Teel. "Five Top Challenges Affecting Healthcare Leaders in the Future." Retrieved from https://www.beckershospitalreview.com/hospital-management-administration/five-top-challenges-affecting-healthcare-leaders-in-the-future.html

Jim Thomas. "Understanding Political Risk." *Leaders*, July 2015.

Michael Treacy and Fred Wiersema. *The Discipline of Market Leaders.* Boston, MA: Addison-Wesley, 1995.

Laura Troyani. "Ten Quick and Easy Ways to Begin Organizational Change." *Business Insurance Magazine*, June 22, 2018.

UKEssays. "Operational Management Approaches by Shell Company." Retrieved from https://www.ukessays.com/essays/business/operational-management-approaches-by-shell-company-business-essay.php?vref=1

Dinesh Venkateswaran. "A Critique of Kotter's 8 Step Model for Leading Change, Part 1." Retrieved from https://dineshvenk.wordpress.com/2014/05/19/kotter-critique-part-1/

Dora Wang. "4 Examples of Companies that Nailed Organizational Change." *Business Growth*, August 2016.

The World Economic Forum. *Drivers of Change.* Cologny, Switzerland: The World Economic Forum, 2016.

Martin Zwiling. "6 Management Changes that will Transform Your Business Culture." Retrieved from https://www.inc.com/martin-zwilling/6-management-changes-that-will-transform-your-business-culture.html

Acknowledgement

Capturing Change: Creating Systems of Transformation through Continuous Improvement was made possible by my devoted colleagues at Cuyahoga Community College, whose hard work served as both the inspiration and substance for the book. Through every opportunity and challenge, especially the COVID-19 pandemic, their actions were heartfelt, immediate, and ongoing—just like continuous improvement. I thank them and extend sincere appreciation to the team in Integrated Communications—Jenny Febbo, Eric Wheeler, and Deborah Benz—for their help in preparing the manuscript for publication.

The task of editing went to my good friend and former colleague David Hoovler. He provided the clarity that made more tangible my belief in organizational transformation through enduring change.

As always, my family and friends were ever present, providing moral support and encouragement throughout the production of *Capturing Change*. I am grateful at all times for their patience and love.